AMERICAN COLLEGES

The Uncertain Future

Edited by William P. Lineberry

THE REFERENCE SHELF
Volume 47   Number 3

THE H. W. WILSON COMPANY   •   New York   •   1975

THE REFERENCE SHELF

The books in this series contain reprints of articles, excerpts from books, and addresses on current issues and social trends in the United States and other countries. There are six separately bound numbers in each volume, all of which are generally published in the same calendar year. One number is a collection of recent speeches; each of the others is devoted to a single subject and gives background information and discussion from various points of view, concluding with a comprehensive bibliography. Books in the series may be purchased individually or on subscription.

Library of Congress Cataloging in Publication Data

Main entry under title:

American colleges.

    (The Reference shelf ; v. 47, no. 3)
    Bibliography: p.
    1. Universities and colleges--United States.
I. Lineberry, William P. II. Series.
LA227.3.A397   378.73   75-19005
ISBN 0-8242-0571-5

PREFACE

The turbulent sixties have passed into history. But the calm that has fallen over most of the nation's college campuses today could well be the lull before another storm. Faced with shrinking enrollments, rising costs, and what appears to be a thoroughly shattered nervous system, America's institutions of higher learning are still "up against the wall," and their current problems seem to be growing instead of decreasing. Despite the rush of recent reforms—in some cases, perhaps, because of them—the future has become as uncertain for *alma mater* as for her growing ranks of jobless graduates.

Battered by inflation and recession, middle-class parents find tuition costs soaring out of reach. Stung by the riotous exhibitions of certain student crusaders, state legislators are finding "better" uses for public funds beyond the groves of academe. And faced, for the first time in many years, with half-empty classrooms and too many teachers, colleges are reflecting anew on their role and purpose in what is said to be the most education-conscious country in the world.

In such a climate, the concerns and catchwords of the sixties begin to ring somewhat hollow. "Relevant" now means the kind of specific training that will ensure a job on graduation, not the appropriateness of a given course to the political and social needs of society. Grades, once scorned as symbols of elitism and authoritarian structuring, are again coveted as the necessary means of entry into professional and graduate schools. Student participation in the administration of higher education, like participation in just about any form of administration, has become almost as boring in practice as it seemed exciting in theory.

All of this is not to say that the reforms of the sixties have

3

proved wholly transient. As various articles in this compilation suggest, many of the innovations launched in that hectic time have already proved their value. The impression prevails, however, that the sixties mainly *played* at reform—almost, as Professor Charles Frankel suggests in these pages, in the form of a stylized drama. The impression is reinforced by the awareness, now dawning, that the real tasks of reform still lie ahead.

Hard questions are being broached, if not actually answered. Of what value is a college education? Who should go to college and why? Today, fully half the students leaving high school or scheduled to leave high school are shuffling off to college. Does this make sense when 80 percent of the nation's jobs do not require a college degree? Does it make sense when 68 percent of today's upper-income adults do not themselves possess a degree? Is learning to be valued for its own sake or for the way in which it realistically prepares a student for a meaningful contribution to society? If admission standards are lowered to accommodate the disadvantaged, is the value of a degree debased or are we simply moving another step down the road toward the democratization of American education? Or, indeed, are we simply reacting to all those empty classroom seats?

These are among the many questions explored in this compilation. The first section sets the stage, detailing the evolution of the American system of higher education and setting forth in broad outline the key issues and problems confronting that system today. The second section focuses on the major immediate crisis—college finances, the way in which they have been deteriorating and the solutions being proposed to right them. Section III explores the sometimes contradictory efforts underway in the struggle for reform—a struggle, be it noted, which still arouses healthy passions despite the wearying and raucous trials of recent years. The last two sections attempt to capture the current mood and attitudes of those most directly involved—today's students, professors, and college administrators.

The compiler wishes to thank the authors and publishers who have courteously granted permission for the reprinting of their materials in this book.

WILLIAM P. LINEBERRY

May 1975

A NOTE TO THE READER

The reader's attention is directed to past Reference Shelf issues dealing with problems in American education, and in particular: *Colleges at the Crossroads* (Volume 37, Number 6) and *New Trends in the Schools* (Volume 39, Number 2), both edited by this compiler, and *Turmoil on the Campus* (Volume 42, Number 3), edited by Edward J. Bander. Each provides earlier background material for any reader interested in further pursuit of the subject.

CONTENTS

PREFACE 3

I. HIGHER EDUCATION IN TRANSITION

Editor's Introduction 11
William W. Brickman. Looking Backward ....
.... Annals of the American Academy of Political
and Social Science 12
Martin Mayer. The Legacy of Change ...... Fortune 28
Ronald Berman. Beneath the Surface Calm ....
.... New York Times Magazine 45
Old Myths, New Realities . Better Homes and Gardens 56

II. THE COST CRUNCH

Editor's Introduction 65
Committee for Economic Development. Dimensions of
the Financial Crisis 66
Larry Van Dyne. Soaring Tuition .... New Republic 70
The Scramble for Athletes .... New York Times 76
Caroline Bird and Stephen G. Necel. Is It Worth the
Price? .... Esquire 82
On the Average, It's Worth It .... U.S. News &
World Report 90
Paul Woodring, Who Should Go to College? ....
.... Educational Digest 92

III. THE STRUGGLE FOR REFORM

Editor's Introduction 98
Ghosts of the Sixties ...... U.S. News & World Report   99
Charles Frankel. Reforming the Reforms ... Daedalus 104
Martin Mayer. Open Admissions for All? ....
.... Commentary 119
James Cass. Reforming the Curriculum ....
.... Saturday Review/World 145

IV. THE NEW STUDENT MOOD ON CAMPUS

Editor's Introduction 149
Stephen R. Weissman. Pulling Down the Barricades ..
.... Nation 150
Iver Peterson. Return of the Work Ethic ....
.... New York Times 159
James L. Morrison and Scott Anderson. A New Sexual
    Ethic? .... Education Digest 165
Edward B. Fiske. Hazing No, Community Service Yes
.... New York Times 168

V. FACULTY AND ADMINISTRATORS

Editor's Introduction 174
Harold L. Enarson. Authority's Thin Red Line ......
.... Vital Speeches of the Day 175
Donald Light, Jr. Accent on Teaching ..... Daedalus 182
Mary Costello. The Struggle Over Tenure ....
.... Editorial Research Reports 192

Frederick L. Redefer. A Program for the Future . . . . . .
. . . . Saturday Review/World 200

BIBLIOGRAPHY 207

I. HIGHER EDUCATION IN TRANSITION

EDITOR'S INTRODUCTION

Things are changing in higher education, and not, it would seem, for the better. The starkest fact is, as usual, an economic one: the "baby boom" of the fifties is over; by 1990 there will be half a million fewer students emerging from high school and heading for college than there are today. The base of higher education is shrinking, not only because of a drop in the birthrate but because of an evident disinclination of growing numbers of eligible students to extend their education. As with everything else, on the other hand, the costs are rising.

On all sides, therefore, a reevaluation of higher education is now underway—by economists of its finances, by students of its value, by teachers of its content, and by society of its purpose. The past is being scrutinized for clues to future directions. As the first article in this section indicates, varying long-term trends have been shaping the structure and content of American higher education since the founding of Harvard College in 1636. These trends provide the broad context in which future directions will be decided.

Yet it is the urgent and pressing needs discussed in the following two articles that will have immediate impact on higher education's future course. Each is written by a concerned student of the subject—the first article by the author and editor Martin Mayer and the second by the administrator Ronald Berman—and both reflect a disquieting concern with the legacy of the disruptive sixties. The underlying tone of pessimism suggests that, having sown the wind, our colleges and universities must now perforce reap the whirlwind. Even if financial problems can be resolved, hard times may still lie ahead.

However complex the current problems, their solution is

not aided by the myths and misconceptions about colleges in general that prevail in the popular mind. The last article in this section is therefore a commonsensical guide to some basic facts about American colleges today.

LOOKING BACKWARD [1]

Higher education in the Western Hemisphere was first suggested in 1538 by the authorization by Papal bull of the University of Santo Domingo. Beginning with the actual opening of the Royal and Pontifical University of Mexico in 1553, higher educational institutions made their appearance in that century and in the early part of the following century in Peru, Guatemala, Colombia, and Argentina. Thus, the university in the New World was not an Anglo-Saxon discovery.

One reason for the delay in the establishment of higher education in the English colonies was the noncooperative attitude of the Indians, who with the massacre of 1622 aborted the Henrico College project in Virginia. Undaunted, the English came back in 1624 with a plan for an *Academia Virginiensis et Oxoniensis*—loosely translatable as "Oxford-in-Virginia"—but this never came into being. Oxford and Cambridge were the models for the inauguration of higher learning in America with the founding of Harvard College in 1636. The aims, administration, atmosphere, and academic work in the nine colonial colleges were, for the most part, under the control of churches and in line with the spirit of religious tradition. Secularism reared its head, as did modernism, around the mid-eighteenth century in response to the winds of the Enlightenment, skepticism, ma-

[1] From "Higher Education in Historical Perspective," by William W. Brickman, professor of educational history and comparative education, Graduate School of Education, University of Pennsylvania. *Annals of the American Academy of Political and Social Science.* 404:31-43. N. '72. Copyright © 1972 by The American Academy of Political and Social Science. All rights reserved. Reprinted by permission.

terialism, and scientism sweeping westward across the Atlantic.

There were signs of change in the late colonial and early republican periods: instructions in law, medicine, engineering, modern languages, and social subjects; and the beginnings of the state university movement in Georgia, North Carolina, and Vermont. Public and private institutions were promoted by the Dartmouth College decision handed down in 1819 by the United States Supreme Court, which prevented the state from unilaterally changing the charter of a higher institution. The nineteenth century saw the emergence of colleges for women, coeducational schools, and professional education and training in dentistry, agriculture, military skills, and business. The rise of commerce and industry, the dissemination of Darwinism, intellectual contacts with the European continent, the geographic growth of the nation, and other factors led to the inclusion of new content in the collegiate curricula: more sciences, psychology, sociology, literary history, linguistics, pedagogy, political science, and so forth. The elective plan introduced at Harvard, the graduate program on the European plan inaugurated in 1876 at the Johns Hopkins University, the expansion of the land-grant universities as a consequence of the Morrill Acts of 1862 and 1890, the launching of university presses and scholarly journals, the beginnings of accreditation of colleges and universities, the growing popularity of intercollegiate athletics, and the establishment of facilities for advanced learning by Negroes were among the developments which characterized higher education in America by 1900.

The early part of the twentieth century was marked by the establishment of the junior (now community) college, the activities of the College Entrance Examination Board, the revolution in medical education as a result of the devastating report in 1910 by Abraham Flexner, and the founding of the American Association of University Professors. Criticism of the various aspects of higher education—curriculum, students, faculty, administration—was by no means rare in the nineteenth century; in the twentieth, it became a common custom. Upton Sinclair, Irving Babbitt, Abraham Flexner, Robert Maynard Hutchins, Jacques Barzun, and Harold Taylor represent a small number of critics whose ideas circulated in academia and society.

The American college and university changed as never before during the quarter-century following World War II. The GI Bill of Rights and its successors, the wartime baby boom, the growth of the community colleges, the impact of the United States Commission on Civil Rights and the United States Supreme Court decisions, the advancing affluence, and the international exchange programs brought about an enrollment explosion and diversification. As statistics skyrocketed, an activistic student movement forced the recognition of new concepts in admission, curriculum, evaluation, and governance in higher education. There exists at this time an uncertainty as to the future in college and university circles. The concerns are many, with few so immediately pressing as the dwindling of the dollar.

Such, in brief, is the skeleton sketch of three centuries or more of higher education in the United States. What follows is an effort at elucidating some major characteristics and themes against the background of time. They are, by consonantal coincidence: proliferation, pluralism, pietism, profanation, professionalization, popularization, politicization, parietalization, polarization, polemicization, and peregrination.

Proliferation

The internationally known sociologist of higher education, Professor Joseph Ben-David of the Hebrew University of Jerusalem, begins his recent [1971] study with the statement that "the most conspicuous characteristic of the United States system of higher education is its size." He links this phenomenon with the characteristics of comprehensiveness, equalitarianism, degree differentiation, a standardized conception of degree programs, and integration of the system through interinstitutional transferability. While the last two points may be debatable, there is little doubt of the uniqueness of the quantitative growth. A look into the statistical data compiled annually by the United States Office of Education will be fruitful. From a total of 101 colleges in 1842, there was a great leap forward to 563 in 1869, to 998 in 1889, to 1,409 in 1929, to 2,230 in 1965, and to more than 2,550 in 1971. Faculty increased from 5,553 (including 666 women) in 1869, to 596,400 in 1965, to 758,900 in 1969, of whom 167,400 were women; students increased from 52,286 (11,126 women) in 1869–70 to 6,928,115 (2,089,113 women) in 1968–69. The junior colleges rose from 480 in 1947, to 891 in 1970, with a corresponding increase in enrollment from 222,045 (70,042 women) to 2,209,921 (617,798 women) in 1969. The growth in the percentage of women in relation to men is noteworthy both for faculty and for students. Also interesting is the fact that the collegiate enrollment in 1950 represented 14.2 percent of the total population aged eighteen to twenty-four years, as compared to 32.8 percent in 1971. Somewhat comparable are the data assembled by the Organization for Economic Cooperation and Development. From 1950 to 1965 the percentage of higher education enrollments of the twenty to twenty-four years age group went from 4.6 to 10.1 in West Germany, from 4.8 to 11.9 in the United Kingdom, from 5.7 to 16.8 in France, from 7.9 to 23.7 in Canada, and from 20.0 to 40.8 in the United States. Another indicator is the number of students per 100,000 population: 2,577 in the United States (1964); 1,128 in the Netherlands (1964); 611 in West Germany (1964); and 366 in the United Kingdom (1963). Finally, in considering numbers, one should not overlook the rise in the attendance of foreign students in America—from 34,000 in 1954–55, to 144,708 in 1970–71.

One need not be a sophisticated social statistician to realize that numbers constitute but part of the story. With regard to quality, a foreign observer points out that the ". . . sustained growth in the quantity and level of education was not accompanied by any decline in quality, at least not

as far as the early 1960s." What is important is the evidence
of general accessibility to higher education with a constant
decrease in discrimination toward constituent groups of the
population. In point of actual fact, as Ben-David comments,
"As to race, recent data show that, if anything, there is discrimination in favor of black students in the educational
system." The vast system of higher education, as numerous
critics have shown, has significant and other faults, but a
planned *numerus clausus,* which keeps out those who lack
means or any of the characteristics of the majority of the
population, is not one of them.

Pluralism

The diversification of the student body in the United
States is not a recent phenomenon; it has roots in the remote
past. At a time when religious minorities were barred from
the universities of the dominant faiths—in Oxford and Cambridge, for example, as late as 1872—there were stirrings of
religious pluralism at the College of Rhode Island (Brown
University). According to the charter granted in February
1764 to this institution by the General Assembly, the "Bap-
tists or Anti-Pedobaptists" constituted twenty-two of the
thirty-six trustees, the Quakers and Episcopalians five each,
and the Congregationalists four.

And furthermore, it is hereby enacted and declared, that into this
liberal and catholic institution shall never be admitted any religious tests; but, on the contrary, all the members hereof shall forever enjoy full, free, absolute, and uninterrupted liberty of
conscience; And that the places of Professors, Tutors, and all other
officers, the President alone excepted, shall be free and open for
all denominations of Protestants: And that youth of all religious
denominations shall and may be freely admitted to the equal advantages, emoluments, and honors of this College or University;
and shall receive a like, fair, generous and equal treatment during
their residence therein, they conducting themselves peaceably, and
conforming to the laws and statutes thereof: And that the public
teaching shall, in general, respect the sciences; and that the sec-
tarian differences of opinion shall not make any part of the public
and classical instruction: Although all religious controversies may

be studied freely, examined, and explained by the President, Professors, and Tutors, in a personal, separate, and distinct manner, to the youth of any or each denomination: And above all, a constant regard be paid to, and effectual care taken of, the morals of the College.

Some proselytism is indicated, particularly when the penultimate passage is compared with the corresponding portion in the original draft of the charter, prepared by the Reverend Ezra Stiles, future president of Yale, and presented to the General Assembly of Rhode Island in August 1763. Nonetheless, the later statutes made it abundantly clear that more than lip service was given to religious diversity. Thus, observers of Saturday as the Sabbath were exempt from attending church on Sunday; Friends were allowed to wear their hats on college grounds; and " 'young gentlemen of the Hebrew persuasion' were formally exempted from the operation of the law which commanded, on penalty of expulsion, that no student should deny the divine authority of the Old and New Testaments." Moreover, the records of 1770 indicate that "the children of Jews may be admitted into this institution without any constraint or imposition whatsoever."

The unique charter and statutes of Brown University were fully in accord with the tradition of religious freedom in Rhode Island. However, this precedent of pluralism was to be an innovation without honor for the nation at large until close to the mid-twentieth century. The struggle for equality of opportunity in higher education for religious minorities was a long and arduous one.

Racial Minorities

Also tortuous was the recognition of the needs of the racial minorities—the Indians and the Negroes. Tentative efforts at providing Indians with what might be considered higher education were made in 1618, when Governor-elect George Yeardley of Virginia was instructed by James I to plan a "College for the Children of the Infidels" in conjunc-

tion with Henrico College. A special committee, appointed
the following year, reported in 1621 that funds were available for an East Indy Schoole, which,

... as a Collegiate or free schoole should have dependance vpon
the [Henrico] Colledge in Virginia Wch should be made capable
to recaue Schollers from the Schoole into such Scollerships and
fellowshipps as the said Colledge shalbe endowed withall for the
aduancement of schollers as they arise by degres and deserts in
learninge.

The fate of this attempt has been mentioned on a previous page. More successful, even in a small way, was the
experiment of the Indian College at Harvard in the mid-
seventeenth century. The handful of Indians who were exposed to the higher learning in Cambridge, unfortunately,
were not made of stern stuff: they died either before or after
graduation. The sole Indian alumnus of colonial Harvard
was Caleb Cheeshahteaumauk (1665), who managed, through
a Latin epistle, to convince the contributors of funds to the
college of the soundness of their educational investment.
Addressing Robert Boyle, the scientist, and the *"honoratis-
simi benefactores . . . O terque, quaterque ornatissimi, aman-
tissimi viri,"* he praised their great generosity in providing
support *"propter educationem nostram; et ad sustentationem
corporum nostrorum."*

The question of educating Indians was more involved
than the matter of missionary work, as was clear from the
incident narrated by that very clever man, Benjamin Franklin. Writing on "The Savages of North America," he made
this perceptive observation: "Savages we call them because
their manners differ from ours, which we think the perfec-
tion of civility; they think the same of theirs." He then
proceeded to illustrate this idea of cultural relativism by the
following tale:

An instance of this occurred at the treaty of Lancaster, in
Pennsylvania, *anno* 1744, between the government of Virginia and
the Six Nations. After the principal business was settled, the com-
missioners from Virginia acquainted the Indians by a speech that

there was at Williamsburg a college, with a fund for educating Indian youth; and that, if the Six Nations would send down half a dozen of their young lads to that college, the government would take care that they should be well provided for, and instructed in all the learning of the white people. It is one of the Indian rules of politeness not to answer a public proposition the same day that it is made; they think it would be treating it as a light matter, and that they show it respect by taking time to consider it, as of a matter important. They therefore deferred their answer till the day following; when their speaker began, by expressing their deep sense of the kindness of the Virginia government, in making them that offer; "for we know," says he, "that you highly esteem the kind of learning taught in those colleges, and that the maintenance of our young men, while with you, would be very expensive to you. We are convinced, therefore, that you mean to do us good by your proposal, and we thank you heartily. But you, who are wise, must know that different nations have different conceptions of things; and you will therefore not take it amiss, if our ideas of this kind of education happen not to be the same with yours. We have had some experience of it; several of our young people were formerly brought up at the colleges of the northern provinces; they were instructed in all your sciences; but when they came back to us they were bad runners, ignorant of every means of living in the woods, unable to bear cold or hunger, knew neither how to build a cabin, take a deer, nor kill an enemy, spoke our language imperfectly, were therefore neither fit for hunters, warriors, nor counsellors; they were totally good for nothing. We are however not the less obliged by your kind offer, though we decline accepting it; and, to show our grateful sense of it, if the gentlemen of Virginia will send us a dozen of their sons, we will take great care of their education, instruct them in all we know, and make *men* of them."

Taking this account at face value, then, it would seem that the students of the College of William and Mary could have received a higher form of education among the Indians than at home. In any event, a system of intercultural exchange might have been desirable.

Still on the subject of Indians, since they are, in all probability, the most disadvantaged of the contemporary minorities with regard to higher educational opportunities, it is fitting to recall the Dartmouth experiment. The charter granted in 1769 by King George III specified that Dartmouth College was intended "for the education and instruction of Youth of the Indian Tribes in this land in reading, writing and all parts of learning which shall appear necessary and expedient for civilizing and christianizing Children of Pagans as well as in all liberal Arts and Sciences; and also of English youth and any others." Later on, the charter, in empowering the trustees to enact regulations, enjoined them from

... excluding any Person of any religious denomination whatsoever from free and equal liberty and advantage of Education or from any of the liberties and privileges or immunities of the said College on account of his or their speculative sentiments in Religion and of his or their being of a religious profession different from the said Trustees of the said Dartmouth College.

Was this an echo of the Brown charter? At any rate, here are some beginnings of the pluralistic policy that characterized American higher education in times to come. If theory outpaced practice, this is evidence of human, not particularly national, frailty.

On the subject of the higher education of minorities, that of the Negro should command considerable attention. "The year 1676 [was selected by the historian Horace Mann Bond] as the first beginning of Negro higher education in the Northern Americas," but the effort was tentative at best. Then came the tutoring of selected young Negroes, John Chavis for example, under the Reverend John Witherspoon, president of the College of New Jersey (Princeton University). During the four decades or so until the Civil War, there were fewer than a score of black graduates of American colleges, most of them from the hospitable halls of Oberlin College. The pioneers were Edward Jones (Amherst College, August 1826), future principal of Fourah Bay Christian Institution in Sierra Leone, and John B. Russwurm (Bowdoin College, September 1826), who also served as educator, editor-publisher, and governor in Liberia. One recognizably higher institution for Negroes, Wilberforce University in Ohio, finally came into being in 1856.

With the peace of Appomattox came increased opportunities in the form of institutions for Negroes: Atlanta University, 1865; Lincoln University, 1866 (Ashmun Institute, 1854); Howard University, 1867; Hampton Normal and Agricultural Institute, 1868; and Tuskegee Normal and Industrial Institute, 1881. Tuskegee and its president, Booker T. Washington, became well-known among European educators in the early twentieth century for the progressive idea and practice of combining academic with technical work.

All this Negro higher education may have been on a segregated basis, but it was accessible as never before in American history. In addition, the doors were to open before long in the state universities, in the North at least. Thus, the Second Morrill Act of 1890 for the further endowment of land-grant colleges stipulated:

That no money shall be paid out under this act to any State or Territory for the support and maintenance of a college where a distinction of race or color is made in the admission of students, but the establishment and maintenance of such colleges separately for white and colored students shall be held to be a compliance with the provisions of this act if the funds received in such State or Territory be equitably divided as hereinafter set forth . . .

This act represented both a drive for integrated and a legal tolerance of segregated higher education, as well as a precursive principle of what was soon to be constitutionally recognized as the separate-but-equal doctrine. However, the events of the next half-century were to uphold the minority opinion of Associate Justice John Marshall Harlan: "Our Constitution is color-blind, and neither knows nor tolerates classes among citizens." The weakening of racial segregation in higher education began with the admission, by order of the Maryland Court of Appeals in 1936, of Donald Murray, a black alumnus of Amherst College, to the University of Maryland Law School. The next three decades witness the withering away of most, if not all, of the disabilities that prevented the blacks from access to higher education. *Tem-*

pora mutantur, nos et mutamur in illis [Times change and we change with them].

From Pietism to Profanation

The history of higher education in America reveals a profound change in purpose, personnel, and curriculum, from the policy of pristine piety of the Puritans to the secularistic, not infrequently antireligious situation in many contemporary institutions. Compulsory chapel and religion, selective denominational admissions, and other practices favoring a particular faith or religious grouping have tended to disappear. Churches have given up control of institutions traditionally identified with their doctrines, whether because of financial crisis or on account of turbulence within the tribe. Neither Protestantism, nor Catholicism, nor Judaism has been spared the slipping from the sacred to the secular. In the *Zeitgeist* of the 1970s, the spiritual heterogeneity of higher education seems to lack "relevance.". . .

At the present time, it is plainly evident that American higher education has but a vestige of its original religious character. The church colleges of today are "in most cases colleges first and church-related second." The diminishing impact of religion and church in higher education of the 1970s is evidence of the gradual disappearance of the image of the past and of the emergence of the new secularistic characteristic of the American college and university.

Professionalization

The early American college, as exemplified by Harvard and Yale, had as a basic purpose the education of ministers. The picturesque language of *New England's First Fruits* (1643) comes at once to mind. This pamphlet, which publicized the offerings and needs of Harvard College to the public in England, stated that, after the colonists settled down in the New World, "One of the next things we longed for and looked after was to advance *Learning* and perpetuate it to Posterity; dreading to leave an illiterate Ministery to the Churches, when our present Ministers shall lie in the Dust." It is clear from the subsequent history of Harvard and of the other colonial colleges that the ministry was not the sole profession practiced by the alumni.

What the colonial and later colleges aimed at was not only the professions—that is, the ministry, medicine, law, engineering, education, dentistry, business, and so forth—but also general education or the liberal arts along with the specialty. There were special professional schools, such as the Litchfield Law School, Andover Theological Seminary, Castleton Medical College, the Baltimore College of Dentistry, and the New York College for the Training of Teachers; but these, as a general rule, expected some general education from the candidates for admission. This educational foundation became a necessity for any institution desiring to gain the recognition of university-level standing.

In the course of time, a controversy developed with regard to the relative position of the liberal arts to professional studies in the college. The upholders of learning for its own sake and for general humanistic values were challenged increasingly by those dedicated to the realities of the emerging sciences, social sciences, and technology. With the growing influence of modernism in higher education, some areas of study, especially the classical subjects, began to dwindle in the number of registrants and in curricular significance.

At least one well-known effort was made early in the nineteenth century to erect a wall of separation between liberal education and professional training in the college. The Yale faculty report of 1828 proclaimed that "professional studies are designedly excluded from the course of instruction at college, to leave room for those literary and scientific acquisitions which, if not commenced there, will, in most cases, never be made." More succinctly, "A liberal, is obviously distinct from a professional, education."

Exactly a century later, in his Oxford lectures of 1928 and in the book embodying them, Abraham Flexner upheld the liberal and scholarly status of higher education: "Assuredly neither secondary, technical, vocational, nor popular education belongs in a university." In the professional schools, he accepted the fields of law and medicine as learned areas, but not denominational religion, business education, journalism, and similar subjects.

One of the apparent immediate echoes was the demand by Robert Maynard Hutchins that the university aim at "the cultivation of the intellect" and "the pursuit of truth" for their own sakes. He criticized vigorously the rampant vocationalism and professionalism as "ruinous" to the future of the university as a house of higher learning. Somewhat gloomily, he admitted several years later that the prevailing practices and theories were antithetical to his. The persistence of such movements, he was convinced, spelled future disaster: "The cults of skepticism, presentism, scientism, and anti-intellectualism will lead us to despair, not merely of education, but also of society."

And so the battle continued and still continues. The forces fought by Flexner and others sit securely in the saddle. More of the fields constituting the liberal arts, such as the foreign languages, are on the defensive and decline. Instant practicality has been supplemented with a rigorous definition of "relevance" among the rebellious ranks of faculty and students. Those still addicted to academic values as the core and distinguishing characteristic of higher education are hopefully holding on.

On the positive side, professionalism in higher education has contributed to socioeconomic mobility of minority students and other disadvantaged individuals. In seeking to set up standards, the idea of professionalism has encouraged another feature of American higher education, that of voluntary accreditation of schools and programs. It may be an ill winde, as some insist, but it bloweth some persons "to good."

Popularization

Reference has been made earlier in this essay to the regular rise in registration, over the decades, in colleges and universities. To the extent that the doors are kept open to those who are capable and ambitious—and now even to individuals who are not—the popularization of higher education is a firm step toward democratization. During the past three centuries, gradually but definitively, the walls of distance from, and discrimination toward, religious, ethnic, and racial minorities came down. Women found their place in separate and in coeducational institutions. At the present time, there is action toward equalization of faculty status of men and women. It is apparent that the American college and university are moving in the direction of a level of higher education which is universal in the sense that it is accessible to literally anyone with basic academic ability and ambition. With the adoption of the open admission plan by the City University of New York, it is possible for a person with moderate scholastic skill to advance academically with the aid of additional help [See "Open Admissions for All?" in Section III, below.]

Among the historical developments contributing to the democratic expansion of opportunity were the founding of the municipal colleges, the land-grant institutions, the state university systems, the National Youth Administration during the recovery from the economic depression of the 1930s, the GI Bill of Rights, the provision of fellowships and scholarships in the 1950s and 1960s, and the work-study plan. A fundamental contribution by the land-grant colleges and universities was the education of "capacity enrollments with . . . varied origins, backgrounds, and aims and interests. . . ." At the Iowa State College, "there has been no distinction or discrimination of race or creed in admission or in participation in any of the scholastic or extracurricular programs." There is little reason to believe that this was not typical of most such institutions. As summed up by . . . [two scholars of the subject], "Not only was the United States thus going farther than most other nations in modern times in extending opportunities in higher education to people of every race, of every creed, and of every economic group; it was also in advance in eliminating ancient barriers due to sex." However, there is still room for considerable improvement. One observer complained that, in Pennsylvania, "higher education was essentially class education, reserved largely for those who could afford its costs"; but he also pointed out that "there has been a growing tendency, of relatively recent origin, to spread the benefits of higher education more widely." With an increase in financial aid to students, it may be possible for American higher education to attain the nineteenth century ideal of "a system of free public education extending from the elementary school to the university."

The Other Five "P's"

... Politicization refers to ideological pressures of various kinds upon the trustees, administration, faculty, and students in the colleges and universities. These pressures are often underscored by the power of the purse and of the press. Academic freedom was slow in developing in the United States, as it was elsewhere, including in the classic land of *akademische Lehr- und Lernfreiheit* [academic freedom to teach and to study]. The history of American higher education is full of cases of infringement of the freedom of professors and students, both within the college and *extra muros*. Professor Edward A. Ross was dismissed in 1900 from Stanford University for his socioeconomic views, and Professor John R. Commons in 1896 from Indiana University for his unacceptable economic philosophy. On the other hand, the right of Professor Richard T. Ely to hold his socioeconomic heresies was upheld in 1894 by the University of Wisconsin Board of Regents' ringing report in favor of the encouragement of "that continual and fearless sifting and winnowing by which alone the truth can be found." Also on behalf of academic freedom was the valiant defense in 1903 of Professor John S. Bassett by President John C. Kilgo of Trinity College (now Duke University) against southern racial prejudice. The profession's battle for academic freedom was joined in 1915, when the newly founded American Association of University Professors issued its General Declaration of Principles with its warning that "there are no rights without corresponding duties."

Politicization is linked to polemicization by the various parties concerned with the controversies in higher education. The writings are in abundance and on both sides of the belt. The argumentation, name-calling, and tactics did not always conform to the canons of scientific research and the customs of benevolent human relations. Also connected with these characteristics are parietalization and polarization. The successful struggle by students and their supporters on the campus for the abolition of the policy of *in loco parentis* and all parietal regulations was related to the movement for the aggrandizement of student power. The colleges and universities are no longer what they were, and there is no assurance that further change may not take place, though in which direction one may not prophesy with impunity.

Finally, there is peregrination, the migration of individual ideas and of institutions in various directions across international frontiers and oceans. American higher education has been enriched by other countries throughout its history, and it has also had an impact, for better or for worse, on universities in countries all over the globe. The processes of borrowing, lending, donating, and transplanting have conferred upon many American colleges and universities a cosmopolitan complexion.

THE LEGACY OF CHANGE [2]

Just the other day higher education was an explosive growth sector in the American economy. From 1950 to 1970, the number of students in college more than tripled, and total expenditures rose ninefold. Because the demand for places in college necessarily relates to the birthrate eighteen years earlier, the baby boom of the 1950s seemed to guarantee continuation of the rising trend.

Raw birth figures told only part of the story: every year a higher proportion of the eighteen-year-old-age cohort was completing high school, and a higher proportion of the high school graduating class was moving on to some form of college. Through unprecedented fund-raising drives in the private sector, through bond issues and legislated appropriations in the public sector, the colleges and universities equipped themselves to handle the flood.

Now the wave is cresting; there are almost a third of a million more eighteen-year-olds in the country today than there were in 1970—but suddenly they aren't going to college. Educational statistics are almost as unreliable as crime figures, but the best estimate seems to be that the number of freshmen enrolled in 1973 was below the record numbers of 1970, and nobody is looking for much of an increase this fall. Something like 150,000 places may be vacant. Moreover, colleges must expect a continuing decline in the numbers of new freshmen, for the American birthrate dropped perceptibly through the 1960s and then dramatically in the early 1970s. The number of live births in the United States each year now runs more than 25 percent below the numbers of babies delivered in the late 1950s.

While the birthrate has been dropping, the drive to keep everyone in school to the age of eighteen has lost much of it old force: last year the Kettering Foundation's National

[2] From "Everything Is Shrinking in Higher Education," by Martin Mayer, author of The Schools, authority on trends in higher education. Fortune. 90:122-5+. S. '74. Reprinted by permission of Curtis Brown, Ltd. Copyright © 1974 Time Inc.

Commission on the Reform of Secondary Education (of which I was a member) recommended an end to compulsory education beyond the age of fourteen. In the politics of the debate, the radicals' efforts to "de-school society" work in tandem with the conservatives' efforts to control social-welfare budgets.

Educators are still unable to face up to the dimensions of the shrinkage they must expect in their markets. The Office of Education has been consistently high in its estimates of the size of the high school graduating class five years down the road. Even now, few academic administrators realize—let alone accept—the fact that the three million-plus high school graduates from whom the colleges now recruit will shrink to at most 2.5 million by 1990. Fortunately, 1990 is still a long way off.

No Teachers Need Apply

The first shocks of the demographic earthquake have already damaged the foundations of the teacher-training programs around which many colleges and universities are built. Until recently, one third of all American college graduates (more than one half the females) got their first jobs as teachers. Now, with the number of schoolchildren diminishing year by year, the demand for new teachers in elementary and secondary schools has dropped from a peak of roughly 220,-000 to perhaps 175,000 a year. Inevitably, though not without a struggle, the colleges of education are being reorganized on a smaller scale. Recession has already struck the graduate schools of arts and sciences. Their fate had been grimly cast as long ago as 1965 in a once controversial article by Allan M. Cartter, then a vice president of the American Council on Education [ACE] who demonstrated that in the 1980s the demand for new Ph.D.s within the academic community was likely to fall below zero. As late as 1970, the Office of Education was still projecting more than 475,000 Ph.D.s to be awarded in this decade by American universities; now the likely number is something under 350,000.

Several of the nation's largest and best graduate schools have made heroic reductions. Columbia, for example, has cut back the entrants to its graduate faculties of arts and sciences from almost 1,100 students in 1969 to fewer than 750 this fall. Several state departments of education have proclaimed a moratorium on new Ph.D. programs at universities under their supervision. But most colleges and universities—even the hard-pressed colleges of education—have dug their feet into a philosophy of growth and their heads into the sand. A recent report sponsored by the Council of Graduate Schools argues that "the current of expansion has regularly renewed itself and has remained, historically, the dominant current. Those persuaded by recent setbacks that its reversal is imminent appear to us oblivious to the deepest American aspirations."

The Carnegie Commission on Higher Education, reporting in the early 1970s, took growth to be an inevitable factor in planning for the colleges. "Our educators," says sociologist Robert J. Havighurst of the University of Chicago, "have been inexcusably expansionist, regardless of demographic realities."

Outrunning the Capacity to Pay

Just the maintenance of the higher-education enterprise at anything like its present size will require either a considerable growth in expenditure per student or the recruitment of an ever growing proportion of each ever shrinking age cohort. The first alternative seems very unlikely. At the private colleges, tuition charges (over $2,000 a year almost everywhere; over $3,000 at the "best" schools) have outrun the capacity of middle-class parents to pay. At the public colleges, state legislators are becoming increasingly insistent on efficiency, performance, "accountability." Faced with a shrinking, price-elastic demand, higher education can hold its own only by expanding the market it serves.

On the surface, it is hard to see how this task can be accomplished. Half of each adolescent-age cohort—more than government agencies have eased off on formal educationa[l] requirements for informal jobs. But the trend lines still poin[t] the other way: more and more occupations are being reclassi[-] fied to require a college degree for entry. "Credentialism," t[o] use the label first employed by the sociologist S. M. Miller, i[s] a besetting vice of bureaucratized societies. . . .

Tutoring Shops at Harvard

The second caveat to the cry of alarm about standard[s] is that the word "standards" carries a spurious connotation of permanence. A college diploma from almost any rea[l] college undoubtedly certifies more than such a documen[t] did fifty years ago, when Oxford and Cambridge gave "pass degrees" to students who never took any exams, and Mount Auburn Street in Cambridge, Massachusetts, was lined with commercial tutoring operations that sold Harvard students term papers and sample answers for exam questions that certain professors were known to ask year after year.

Long before phrases like "open admissions" were bandied about, several of the land-grant universities in the Midwest were required by law to accept any graduate of the state's high schools. It may well be that most colleges expect less from students today than they did half a dozen years ago; but they would have to retrogress quite a ways before their demands diminished to the levels that were common a generation back.

The third caveat is that there really *is* something to the argument that attendance at college has a civilizing effect. Over the years, professional baseball players have been re- cruited mostly from sandlots and high schools, while pro- fessional football players are almost always veterans of four years at college. Sportswriters who regularly visited both were always impressed at how much more vulgar and vicious life was in the baseball dressing rooms.

At a cost that probably tops $400 million, New York's City University [CUNY] now enrolls about 140,000 full-time day students, including at least 10,000 who read on a junior-

three fifths of all who are graduated from our high schools— now proceed to some form of "postsecondary education." Among those whose grades place them in the top quarter of the high school graduating class, seven eighths now go on to college; among those in the top half, three quarters continue. Keeping enrollments steady will require in the next ten years the recruitment and retention of very large numbers of stu- dents whose previous academic accomplishments fall below the average of their age group.

Increasing the proportion of weak students in the group, however, necessarily reduces the productivity of the educa- tional dollar. Even today, when so much has been forgotten, most observers recognize that different people take to school- ing with very different quantities of enthusiasm, and profit by it in very different measures. Efficiency calls for the allo- cation of scarce educational resources to those who will benefit most by their employment. Jefferson designed a pub- lic school system for Virginia, through the university level, not to establish a high standard of education for all but to assure that "the best geniuses will be raked from the rubbish annually." There is an inescapable law of diminishing re- turns in the application of educational effort to increasingly marginal students.

Doctrine has held that center-city students are weak be- cause not enough money is spent on their schools as com- pared with the money spent on the suburban schools where the students are strong. A decade's mountain of statistical evidence, however, strongly suggests that increasing expendi- ture on the schools where the weak students are does not significantly improve student performance. Disparities of expenditure prior to the 1960s, when the federal government began to force-feed the urban schools, now appear to have been rational in terms of productivity: the money went where it could be most effectively employed. There are in- deed compelling reasons to spend more money on urban schools, but the educational benefits alone could not justify the costs.

If They Can't Read the Textbooks

Educational arguments resting on economic rationality have recently come to be described as "elitist," a word of somewhat uncertain but clearly pejorative meaning. In advanced circles at the foundations, it is now considered a condemnation of a "sick society" that money is spent on the schooling of those who seek education, enjoy it when found, and use it, rather than on those who shun education, endure it when required, and profit little by it.

And there is some history to support the visionaries. American colleges tripled their enrollment from 1950 to 1970 without significantly reducing the average student's score on the tests used to measure receptivity to academic instruction. Extremely bright adolescents (especially boys) had been sent to college from poor farmhouses and tenements throughout our history, but until this generation, social-class status and family income had been much more important than ability in deciding who went to college and who went to work.

Today, however, the resource of high-potential students not going to college has been virtually depleted. Though there are always pleasant (and unpleasant) surprises when expectations are compared to the subsequent performance of individuals, the groups not now proceeding to higher education are likely to supply only small numbers of students who master any of the established college programs. The productivity of the resources employed to place and hold this population in such programs would be very small—and would, be perceived as very small. (A committee of the Connecticut state legislature grumbled publicly a few weeks ago that the state's community colleges were wasting money on academic courses for students who couldn't read the textbooks.) And the institutions would fall apart from what historians Oscar and Mary Handlin have described as "the frustration of conforming to standards beyond reach."

Thus the colleges and universities need a redefinition of their services that will enable them to recruit weaker students, yet appear as productive as they were when the average ability levels were higher. This task might be manageable. After all, one of the possible measures of productivity is something the colleges control completely: the number of diplomas awarded. And another—increased self-realization by the students—is so vague that nobody can really say for sure whether the emperor does or doesn't have any clothes. Many American colleges are already moving along both of these paths, retaining through to graduation increasing numbers of students who in the old days would have shaken this dust from their feet, and setting out ever more undemanding, "relevant" sweetmeats in their smorgasbord of courses. "The disappearing ingredient in higher education today," says Hofstra University President Robert Payton, "is quality."

Three caveats must be entered.

The first is that the demand for diplomas has been grossly overstimulated by businesses and governments that require specific pieces of paper—rather than some possibly more valid demonstration of ability and attitude—for entry to certain jobs and training programs. The American Council on Education conducts an annual opinion poll of entering freshmen, and in 1971 the poll included a question on why the freshmen had come to college. To "get a better job" led the list of answers by male students. Educational criteria are not necessarily irrelevant to decision making by personnel departments—"A college diploma," President Roger Heyns of the ACE notes mildly, "gives evidence of an ability to learn what will be needed on the job." Still, if the job the student hopes to get can be done perfectly well without mastery of a college program, he cannot be seriously faulted for demanding the required piece of paper whether or not he has done college-level work—and colleges should not be denounced when they provide one.

Under prodding from the Equal Employment Opportunity Commission, and the courts, some corporations are

high-school level. "There are people who want a touch of college," says Alfred A. Giardino, the new chairman of the Board of Higher Education that supervises CUNY. "It opens certain doors. Nothing makes it wrong to allow them that exposure. There's a nonquantifiable element in this even for those at the very bottom."

Still, even after the caveats have made the observer careful, there remain reasons for serious concern. Today's college—with its antisocial littering, the noise level of its stereo systems and transistor radios, the collapse of its organized extracurricular life and "school spirit," the legitimation of violence in its politics—clearly does less than its predecessors to civilize the new generation.

The phenomenon Harvard's David Riesman called "grade inflation" quickly depreciates the useful and perhaps irreplaceable currency of academic accomplishment, and like price inflation, it creates ultimately impossible expectations. There are grounds for concern that the high schools have deteriorated to the point where the average college-bound senior is less prepared for college work than his predecessors were: from the mid-1950s to the mid-1960s, though the numbers taking the test multiplied five times, the average score on the Scholastic Aptitude Test of the College Entrance Examination Board held steady, but in the last decade, the average score has dropped significantly.

And we must look forward to a time when more and more colleges will be scrambling for students.

The Terrifying Graphs

Having spent the better part of a year on commission from the Twentieth Century Fund to explore the feasibility of an international university-entrance examination, I can testify that questions about the reliability and validity of educational certificates are hard to answer anywhere in the world. They become especially painful and complicated in this country because they get mixed up with the national commitment to racial equality, earnestly offered in the 1960s and now eroding in the schools and colleges under the pressures of failure. The blunt fact is that about 13 percent of each age cohort reaching eighteen is black, but in terms of academic achievement as measured by tests, blacks appear to make up only 3 percent of the top half of our high school graduating class.

In the hindsight of half a dozen years, it is hard to understand how so many informed people (myself included) could have underestimated so drastically the dimensions of the job that the schools and colleges had undertaken to accomplish. The argument that the problem was mostly one of social-class status was being used long after the Civil Rights Commission had published in its book *Racial Isolation in the Public Schools* (1967) the terrifying graphs that showed black twelfth-graders from middle-class families with average achievement scores below those of white twelfth-graders who came from working-class families.

One summer, as a member of President [Lyndon B.] Johnson's Panel on Educational Research and Development, I participated briefly in a special program for teachers of freshmen at black colleges, and I remember becoming vastly annoyed with my mostly black audience because their questions reflected so depressed a view of their students. Looking back, it is as though we believed that if we wanted equality, we could buy it: all we needed was goodwill and money.

Attempts to meet workable commitments in a straightforward manner were continuously and subtly sabotaged through these years by a change in popular—and, indeed, professional—perceptions of the social function of higher education in America. Once there was an educational ladder, on which people could climb to higher status and income; now there is a succession of educational hurdles that people must jump before arriving at the end of their rainbow. In the ladder image, the colleges could give a helping hand and a shove upwards; but there could be no blinking the difficult truth that most black students would have to work harder than most white students to achieve comparable results. In the hurdles image, the colleges could take care of everything just by removing the barriers: as representatives of "the white world," they would accept responsibility for black students' deficiencies and promise to make everything come out all right.

When City University in New York developed its Open Admissions program, freedom from flunking was actually written into the plan, which assured that nobody would be dismissed until his or her second (probably third) year. Militants had demanded and the university had agreed that Open Admissions must not be "a revolving door." Students had to figure out for themselves the notion that ultimately they would be rewarded for getting the work done and penalized for failure to do so. Many did figure it out (just because someone finds academic subjects hard does not mean he is a fool), but many did not. And there were always plenty of voices to proclaim that any student's troubles were the result of institutional racism or the fascistic irrelevance of the professoriat.

"For the Educationally Hesitant"

Under the hammer of experience, at City University and at other colleges where large numbers of unprepared students were rapidly ingested, requirements fell one by one— not only the general requirements in English composition, elementary mathematics, and the rudiments of a foreign language, but also (and perhaps more important) the internal institutional requirements that established certain lower-level courses as prerequisites for entering upper-level courses. While the prerequisites system functioned, those who graded students for their performance on the lower levels were in effect recommending them to other members of their department, and were responsible for them to the collegiality of the department. With the elimination of prerequisites, the teachers of the lower-level courses became responsible only to the administration, which had a first commitment to keeping these students at the school and happy.

There were and are colleges that worked at these problems more seriously. In Minneapolis, an established two-year general college functioning within the context of the University of Minnesota established what Esther Wattenberg, director of its New Careers program, called "transitional education for the educationally hesitant," and those who moved on to the four-year program carried an institutional warranty of adequate capacity.

In 1969, when I visited it as part of a study I was making for the Sloan Foundation, Temple University in Philadelphia had the undergraduate college with the largest black enrollment in the United States (though nobody outside Temple knew it). Recruitment to the "Opportunities Program" was managed by a young black graduate student named Otis Smith. He and five colleagues browsed the black neighborhoods of Philadelphia, he said, looking for students who "have done well, or shown steady improvement, in high school, because that's the best predictor. And I check around. You go into the community, and somebody will tell you, 'Well, he's a nice kid—but he doesn't work much, you see him hanging around on the street.' He's out. Or somebody says, 'You can't tell it because he's quiet, but that boy's got it—you give him something to do around the church, he gets it done.' " My impressions as a visitor were that the tone of this enterprise was firm: there was none of the feeling that pervaded some other urban universities, that the institution's mission was becoming one of life support for academic basket cases.

Gilding Self-Images

At most colleges, the arrival of large numbers of black students who performed poorly was a prime cause of grade inflation, one of the few verifiable facts to support a generalized concern about declining standards. Though colleges do not publish their grade-point averages, admissions directors at graduate schools and professional schools see transcripts every year, and the Educational Testing Service for three years has maintained a file of grade records for the 120,000-odd applicants to the nation's law schools who take the Law Schools Admission Test. On the scale of 0 to 4, where C translates to 2, and B translates to 3, the average student at most colleges used to hover about 2.5. Now the *median* grade-point average of college graduates seems to be approaching 2.8, and there are some major schools—Cornell is the most notorious—where it is over 3. Hamilton College, near Cornell, has continued to grade on the old curves, and now feels constrained to send along with every transcript submitted to the admissions department of a graduate school a letter pointing out that 3.1 is still an excellent grade-point average at Hamilton.

Grade inflation is commonly defended on the grounds that higher grades improve a student's self-image, imparting a confidence that is good in itself and very possibly improves his subsequent standard of work. A quick answer is that American college students' self-images are already very positive and do not need further improvement. In a study of the class of 1971 at a sample of ninety-four colleges, researchers found that 25 percent considered themselves in the top 10 percent of their class in scholarship and creativity, 29 percent considered themselves in the top 10 percent for leadership ability, and 57 percent considered themselves in the top 10 percent for responsibility. Raising these self-estimates still higher would seem to be gilding the lily.

The months since the Vietnam cease-fire, which took the intensity out of the student movement, have been perceived by all—with relief or contempt, according to taste—as a time of consolidation and conservatism. Most of the educational reforms born in the assortment of glorious dawns from 1966 to 1970 have already been consigned to the dustheap of history (whence many of them had come).

Fewer courses will be offered this year with a "pass/fail" sanction instead of more discriminating grades, and fewer students will take them: the faculty has learned that offering a pass/fail option does not persuade students to take courses outside their own area of concentration (which was the initial hope), and the students have learned that a record full of pass/fail marks leaves them at the mercy of the standardized test when they apply to graduate or professional school. Fights over "governance" of the college are much less lively now that more students and faculty have learned how time-consuming and dull the tasks of governance are, and how rarely it makes any difference which way a decision goes.

Even the old-fashioned idea that the process of education should produce measurable results has found a new birth of respectability. "The 1960s was the time of the movement against standards," says Executive Vice President Robert J. Solomon of Educational Testing Service, which with two thousand employees is by far the largest educational research operation in the world. "Now there is a movement back. There was a period when people were saying, 'Do away with tests'; now the same people are saying, 'Prove that they're valid.' Competence is important—not many people ever really wanted to give up competence."

The Open University

What has survived and strengthened in the wild garden of educational reforms is the movement toward academic credit for work done in surroundings other than the college classroom. These "nontraditional programs" include plans that award credit for a course on passage of an examination whether or not the candidate was a student somewhere while learning the material; "contract" plans by which students work on their own according to a schedule mapped out with an assigned tutor; and simple or complicated credit-for-experience schemes by which degree candidates are excused some years of college attendance on the grounds that they have already learned on the job what kids learn in the classroom.

The list of purposes that can be served by such devices is almost endless. Both serious interests and trivial desires can be satisfied, while groups that won't or can't make it in traditional surroundings can be given their credentials.

The most fully developed of these programs is Britain's Open University, which uses the resources of BBC radio and television to reach to the homes of some 42,000 matriculated students. The students also read books specially prepared to match the syllabi of the broadcast course, meet at infrequent intervals for seminars at local collection points scattered around the country—and eventually take examinations. Open University courses and exams are by American standards rather stiff. The material has been tried out in the last two years at three universities in the United States: Maryland, Houston, and Rutgers. A forthcoming report on its success here will say, not surprisingly, that the outcomes were very good when the students were both intelligent and highly motivated, much less good when either of these preconditions was absent.

Most nontraditional programs in America are, like Open University, planned for adult education. At New York's Empire State College, which offers neither courses nor facilities and gives credit for independent study performed under contract to tutors, the average age of the 2,100 students is thirty-four. Under the aegis of the University Without Walls [UWW] program based in Yellow Springs, Ohio, however, twenty-six public and private colleges and universities are already offering students of customary college age the option of credit for work done outside.

Whether such programs can flourish in a period when there are empty spaces at established institutions is anybody's guess, and their influence on educational standards could go either way. A couple of years ago, Samuel Baskin, president of the Union for Experimenting Colleges and Universities, which sponsors UWW, would not even consider the argument that identical educational procedures cannot effectively be employed across the full spectrum of his students. UWW serves, among others, deeply but narrowly talented students who insist on working in only one subject, bright self-starters who are bored with college because it involves so much Mickey Mouse, and bewildered slum dwellers who are bored at college because so much of it goes over their heads. To treat them all the same invites fakery. On the other hand, Chicago's Havighurst believes that the end result of the growth of University Without Walls' programs would be "more reliance on external exams, to keep them honest." Like the Regents diploma of the New York high schools, such examinations might come to function as a floor below which deteriorating conventional programs would not be permitted to fall.

IQ Versus Energy

The problem nobody is willing to face is that less structured academic programs, inside or outside the walls, lead to greater gaps between the accomplishments of strong and weak students. Rote memory is an awful way to learn, but it is not discriminatory by social class or race: the tortoise who is willing to do an extra hour of work can outlast the hare who glides along on ability or background. In general, every reduction in curricular or institutional structure reduces the rewards that can be gained by energy and persistence, and increases those that adhere to cultural background and higher IQ. I have no doubt that our best students are emerging from today's less organized higher education with a deeper if not always broader understanding of what they have studied. But despite the egalitarian rhetoric that has accompanied the reform projects, a price is being paid by weaker students whose bewilderment can be masked but not cured by some emotional "commitment"—and whose losses will not be recompensed by a diploma awarded despite their failure to learn much.

The real losers, of course, are those who do learn, who earnestly climb the educational ladder, and then at its top find only the devalued diploma they could have got without all that climbing. Thus the strongest defenders of educational standards are drawn from the community of professors who work at urban universities and have given their lives to improving the futures of the able and ambitious children of the poor—teachers like Sidney Hook, philosopher and old Leftist, who helped organize a nationwide organization of professors called University Centers for Rational Alternatives, as a countervailing force against the revolutionary hoo-ha of the late 1960s. UCRA's executive secretary is Miro Todorovich, a Yugoslav émigré who is a physics professor at Bronx Community College. He has taken a decade's worth of graduates from some of New York's worst high schools and worked with them until he was ready to certify that they could do third- and fourth-year work at City College of New York's demanding and unsentimental College of Engineering.

Todorovich has not been asked to reduce the difficulty of his courses or the extent of his demands, and does not see standards collapsing at his own institution: "We are still less likely to give college credit for high-school-level work than the four-year colleges that have been under so much more political pressure," he says. But in less rigorous fields than physics and less firmly led colleges than Bronx Community, he finds a devaluation of credits and ultimately of diplomas.

There is, of course, a case for pushing additional adolescents into college, and keeping them there as long as the venture makes any sense at all. Educational standards can never be more than cuts in a continuum, statements of probability that this student can in later academic or other work effectively use what he has been taught. Some of those who meet the standards subsequently fail, and some who do not meet them would in fact succeed if given the opportunity. If taxpayers (and parents) are willing to pay the costs of the inefficiencies, it is hard to see why opportunity should not be extended as widely as possible.

Training for Job Opportunities

Chicago's Havighurst sees serious trouble ahead when "CUNY turns out some thousands of bachelor's degrees to people who are not going to get the jobs they expect." But there is even something to be said for training more people than are likely to be employed in the fields for which they are trained, provided they understand the risks.

You can't make long-term academic plans on the basis of man-power projections [says Roger Heyns of the American Council on Education, who was once chancellor of the University of California at Berkeley]. Change the votes of six Senators on the SST, and you wouldn't have had a surplus of engineers at all. If you look at the demand for trained personnel implied in the HEW and environmental programs already on the books, we don't have a surplus of Ph.D.s, we have a shortage. You have to ask yourself why the supply of people to work on energy programs was available when the energy crisis hit. We've been blessed in this country by our concept of abundance.

Unfortunately, abundance achieved by lowering standards of performance can acquire a snowballing momentum. As jobs are redefined to require a college degree for entry, inceasing proportions of the age group demand a college education in self-defense. Diplomas are awarded for lower and lower levels of accomplishment; but, paradoxically, employers intensify their demand for the credentials. A high school diploma is essential today largely *because* so many high school graduates perform so poorly: the argument, never analyzed, is that if the high school graduates are this weak, you certainly can't risk hiring somebody who doesn't even have a high school diploma.

Within the colleges and universities, vital qualities can be drowned by the numbers the enterprise needs so badly. Todorovich speaks scornfully of "the huge growth of the plants that brought in a lot of people who had the attitudes of a simple employee rather than those of a member of a learned profession," and of administrators launching new colleges "who copied programs from other catalogs, then went looking for people to teach just these courses."

Distant observers of American higher education, especially foreign observers, used to be horrified by the surface of football games, fraternities, and beer; but behind that surface, as visitors soon learned, there were sacristies. Today, at colleges where concern for quality gets labeled "elitist," there is nothing sacred. "What gets lost," Todorovich says, "is the veneration for the capacity of the human mind to transcend itself."

Todorovich draws an analogy between the traditional American university and the traditional American drugstore, which offers a giant menu of cheap, mass-produced merchanidse. "When I came," he recalls, "like so many Europeans, I was fascinated by the drugstore, and I was arrogant about it. Then somebody said to me, 'Remember— over in the corner there is somebody certificated who is actually preparing medicine.' But if he goes, then it's no longer a drugstore."

BENEATH THE SURFACE CALM [3]

At the end of the sixties the academic world gratefully welcomed the cessation of violence. It assumed that campus problems were finite and political; with their disappearance, we would be back to normal. The academy hoped for tranquillity and, attaining it, confused it with order. Few realized at the beginning of the seventies that an entirely new set of problems had arisen and that their solution depended on values and traditions that were dealt a staggering blow in the sixties. The traditional university was imperfect but equitable. The same cannot be said of today's.

The seventies began with a shortage of money caused by

[3] From "An Unquiet Quiet on Campus," by Ronald Berman, chairman of the National Endowment for the Humanities. New York *Times Magazine.* p 14+. F. 10, '74. © 1974 by The New York Times Company. Reprinted by permission.

a shortage of public confidence. There have been other external problems: fluctuations in the student population; inflation; changes in federal and state education policies; the sudden constriction of employment. But internal problems are even more severe. We have been left with a politicized environment in which disinterested argument is at a loss. The curriculum is more or less in shreds after its attempts to reflect, with ever increasing speed for most of a decade, the relevancies of the moment. Students are without grades and requirements, while professors are without traditional responsibilities; in both cases there is great anxiety about loss of structure and equity. A new generation of academics has appeared, but, having for some years now argued the superior claims of politics, they find themselves unhappily detained by subjects merely parochial. Innovation, a concept rightly honored when most necessary, has become sterile and mechanical. In the race to attract foundation funds—and because it implies a certain style—innovation has become more of an end than a means. Finally, students are evidently bored by the kind of debate long familiar on campus and are deserting the liberal arts for the vocations in enormous numbers. Because of these issues, the campus is naturally agitated. Because of the difficulty of their solution, it is in a state of anxiety, not to say depression.

The report of the Carnegie Commission states that the universities are undergoing a trauma of self-doubt. Kenneth Clark has written in *The American Scholar* that they have shown an abject failure of nerve. A great variety of such statements on the crisis of confidence in education are now appearing. None of them refer simply to the issues I have just described. They apply to the conditions those issues have both created and encountered. I would put the matter this way: The essential loss of the past decade was not material but moral. The attention of the public was focused on violence, barbarism and physical destruction; what escaped notice was the end of discourse, objectivity and freedom.

Without these, academe is powerless to face the issues and is, in fact, in a state of twittering inertia.

A brief historical review may be useful. There have been two revolutionary changes on campus, one material and the other political. From 1958 to 1968 the American university boomed along with the rest of the economy. There were many benefits as intellectual life became part of the knowledge industry: decent wages and research facilities; *carrière ouverte aux talents;* the end of cultural isolation. But on the whole the experience resembled nothing so much as the effect of the capitalist ethic on medievalism, at least as described by Marx and Engels. If the old campus was paternalistic, the new one was frigidly aloof—there were verifiable stories of students at Berkeley whose only direct contact with their professors was a single annual conversation. Burkeian affection for people, places and institutions disappeared; it was replaced by a freedom easily confused with neglect. The campus atmosphere changed in a way reminiscent of the opening of *Hard Times,* in which the prisons looked like hospitals and the schools looked like prisons. . . .

Problems of the 1970s

The sixties were a time of troubles, but the seventies, far from being their antithesis, are in some respects a continuation. The leading problem is that of the university's mode: dialogue itself. Both as a habit and as one of the components of academic freedom it has been damaged. One of the first to note that life on campus has become tolerant of failure but not of disagreement was Roger Rosenblatt of Harvard, who observed in *The Harvard Alumni Bulletin:*

Much of the faculty has become politicized and politicization is antithetical to its nature. A colleague recently exclaimed how much he had enjoyed a certain dinner party because "everyone there thought exactly the way we do." When intellectual conformity becomes the criterion for success, social or otherwise, the reverberations may eventually be felt in the curriculum, and the university is in trouble.

Tranquillity differs from inertia, which is what now seems to prevail on campus. As Rosenblatt suggests, the former implies healthy opposition, the latter only that difference is unthinkable. Inertia may even imply that the act of discrimination inherent in the power of intelligence is not important. Another member of the Harvard faculty, Martin Kilson, has written in the [New York] *Times* of the importance of a particular debate which was to have taken place at Harvard between Messrs. Shockley and Innis. [Professor William Shockley, a physicist, writes extensively on inherited aspects of intelligence; Roy Innis, a black community leader, has challenged many of his conceptions.—Ed.] While virtually everyone would agree that this debate of itself cannot settle the matter of genetic intelligence, most of those concerned about academic freedom are deeply worried by its cancellation. As Kilson puts it:

These and other actions by faculty members suggest the unfortunate spread of insensitivity toward unfettered discussion at a great institution of higher learning like Harvard. We can now expect more actions of this sort around a number of emotionally charged issues involving blacks, women, homosexuals and Israelis or Jews.

Tranquillity differs not only from inertia but from consensus. It would then be a mistake to interpret the relative quiet of the campus as a sign that its troubles are over. It may simply mean that public debate has been discouraged.

One of the most disturbing cases of enforced consensus has involved the University of California at San Diego. There, a faculty member who ventured to teach, although he did not support, the Jensen hypothesis [linking intelligence and genes] was harassed by a coalition of student groups. Upon appeal to the administration, he was informed that he had only these alternatives: to clear the lectures with his antagonists; to debate them instead of carrying on his lectures; to give up his lectures; to endure harassment. One assumes that the meek shall inherit the earth, but not quite with this kind of encouragement. The effects were demoralizing to the man, his students and his school. And, of course, the effects are felt outside a single locality. As the *Times* editorial of November 23 [1973] said after a similar fiasco at Staten Island Community College: The violent suppression of genetic debate on Staten Island was nothing less than subversion of the Bill of Rights.

Sidney Hook has written of an allied problem of academic freedom at the University of California: the acceptance of censorship in a good cause. *Measure,* the publication of University Centers for Rational Alternatives, observed in its September [1973] issue that any subgroup which feels threatened within a culture may now have recourse to the prohibition of those ideas it finds disagreeable. The Berkeley administration felt, in brief, that research should be discouraged which "may place the reputation or status of a social group or an institution in jeopardy." The implications are such as to make the recent Supreme Court decision on pornography seem Aristotelian. For one thing, the damage to "reputations and self-esteem" liable to be suffered on campus considerably exceeds that permitted by the law of libel! And the truth may in fact be pejorative, so that it is useless to suppress bad news. It is certainly dangerous to give powers to censorial university bureaucracies that we have for generations resisted giving to courts or elected officials.

Threats of this sort relate directly to the degree of public confidence enjoyed by the universities. Legislatures in almost every state have considered (and some have passed) restrictive budgets for university education because they believe that their own values and those of the taxpayers have too long been attacked by the academic world. One's natural instinct is of course to assert that if politicians sincerely believe that partisan values should be taught on campus, or that a single interpretation of American culture should be adopted, or that faculty should be the unthinking spokesmen of a national majority view, then they should be taught the meaning of academic freedom. But if *faculty and administra-*

tors believe that partisan values should be taught on campus
and that a single interpretation of American culture should
prevail or that faculty should be the unthinking spokesmen
of a local majority view, then they too should learn something about academic freedom.

Escape to Utah

Violations of that freedom are generally a matter of
record, but other aggressions and encroachments, perhaps
equally threatening, are diffused through daily life. There
is a superb account of this civility by [the 17th century
British philosopher] Thomas Hobbes: "By manners, I mean
not here decency of behavior; as how one should salute another, or how a man should wash his mouth, or pick his
teeth before company, and such other points of the *small
morals;* but those qualities of mankind that concern their
living together in peace and unity." In fact, what Hobbes
sees as manners we may see as human relationship itself:
the implication of thought and mutual feeling by style. For
a current perception of this, we need not restrict ourselves
to Harvard or the University of California. Far from these
places—at the University of Utah—a new style has been
borne by the winds of doctrine:

A scholar from Michigan, another from California, from
Columbia, or Minnesota now seek a place at Utah. Why? Because
they feel, mistakenly I think, that in our little backwater of academic society we may have preserved, even by accident, some of
the things they loved.... Scholars who would leave greater institutions to come here would hope, somehow, that they might
find again an atmosphere of peace and serenity, perhaps even of
intellectual fair play, although that is wishing for a great deal
now.... But such hopes are romantic dreams.

The writer, Professor Jack Adamson, reflects on a lifetime of teaching he is about to depart. His point, that the
provinces are now more like the capitals of culture than may
be wished, can easily be granted. As he puts it, there is at
least as much floating despair at Utah as at Harvard; and
perhaps the phrase for it might be anomie, which so use-

fully denotes the effect on social structures of personal anxiety. Things are quiet because people do not relate to each other, because the fragile web of cultural assumptions has been broken without being replaced. At Utah (and at a number of places more familiar to me), there is a sterile discord among those who can no longer find neutral ground for disagreement.

The things that Adamson mentions are overly familiar: political righteousness of absolutely Bourbon proportions; the fierce opposition between those who teach their subjects and those who teach things deemed more important; the subversion of academic values and authority; the hypocrisy of moral views so elevated and distant that they make all practical pursuits seem untenable. Perfect righteousness means eventually that nothing human is acceptable.

Some Regressive Innovations

Some of the things I have mentioned were of course characteristic of the sixties; others were made possible by those subsequent changes of assumption that were caused by the sixties. [The writer and social commentator] Irving Kristol has remarked, for example, that obligatory innovation has only just reached the vulnerable smaller schools and secondary systems. It has now become methodologically orthodox—although it was intended to bring about specified changes (some of them necessary) in university study. So what began as an attempt to replace classroom work with other forms, or to illuminate and expand the boundaries of conventional history or biography, was incarnated finally as part of the educational establishment.

It is now *de rigueur* to "innovate" with no regard whatsoever to the necessity. Sometimes, in fact, innovation is regressive. I was recently approached to support the teaching of Leonardo da Vinci in upstate New York secondary schools, a consummation devoutly to be wished. But the method was "innovative"—which is to say that the government would pay some half million dollars for the manufacture of new textual materials able automatically to convey their contents. Knowing the tremendous volume of materials on the subject, their relative cheapness and availability, I had some doubts about the cost and artificiality of the method. It turned out that the reason I had been invited to contribute was intellectual default: The teachers of that district did not themselves want to master Leonardo and hoped that the new materials would teach students without their intervention. Their administrators preferred to ask the government to pay for imbecile "digests" rather than train people properly. I was approached in another case to support "innovative courses" whose principal claim was that they destroyed the old authority of teacher over student. In the new course, everyone taught everyone else, a demonstration of personal independence. That constituted, to our panelists reviewing the grant proposal, a reasonable argument for preserving its financial independence.

I have been approached, in fact, to support an untold variety of projects whose single virtue was novelty. I certainly do not want to claim that in education (as has been said not entirely seriously of theology) originality is a vice. But on the other hand, it is not of itself a cure for ignorance. Some of these projects involved the substitution of the comics for the classics, of the Beatles for Dr. Johnson. If these were proposed in seriousness, so much the worse. But I should think that this replacement is designed to imply that the campus has a good hold on the tail of the *Zeitgeist*. For those uncertain of themselves and anxious for approval, this style passes current for substance.

True innovation allows for greater knowledge. It brings more people into the world of education; it disseminates knowledge to those who need it most; and, with luck, it even converts knowledge to wisdom. It has something to do with method, of course—but it is essentially a matter of substance. When this is forgotten at universities, then we face a real educational loss; to rely on method is to capitulate to fashion.

The loss of substance in the liberal arts is already having demoralizing effects. Teachers unsure of their allegiance are unsure of their professions and of themselves. Students are leaving the liberal arts in droves. At Yale, at Brandeis, at Wright State University (all representative of different points on the spectrum of American education), undergraduates are rushing to vocational or professional studies. Interest in these subjects is understandable, even praiseworthy, but one hopes that this trend is not a reaction to the recent climate of ideological fury and that it is not accompanied by the loss of confidence in the humanistic disciplines. There has of course always been vocationalism on campus. But the new kind has sent students in great numbers to courses which, like economics, seem to provide direct access to security. It may be suggested that although many are rightly interested in the ideas of [economists Milton] Friedman or [John Kenneth] Galbraith, even more are interested in the employment curve of computer technology. One corollary is that few students are interested in values and ethics or, more accurately, in the possibility of coming to terms with them at the university.

The Quest for Equity

For practical purposes there are three forms of equity on campus to consider: the interests of the faculty, those of the students and those of intellectual work itself. The simplest form of equity for faculty is the freedom to conduct classes without inhibition. It is matched by the duty to do so according to those contracts and traditions governing professional life. The contract implies that we teach what we were hired for. The tradition implies that we do it honestly and objectively. And academic freedom implies that we do both of these things in security. As the final report of the Carnegie Commission indicates, the equity of faculty faces severe internal dangers. The commission states in fact that campus judicial procedures ought now to have a dual purpose: "Processes of faculty hearings established in part to protect faculty members from attacks by external powers must now also be capable of protecting the integrity of the campus against those who undertake internal attacks on academic freedom. . . ."

Equity for students involves three main points: the obligation to give them knowledge of the world and themselves; the responsibility of doing so in the form of alternatives rather than of indoctrination; the right they have to competent teaching. There isn't a method in the world that can substitute for competence. And there is no escape from the conclusion that authority must match this responsibility. Authority is not tyranny, but the natural relationship of knowledge to ignorance.

Finally, there is the equity involved in the work and its evaluation. In Steven Cahn's . . . *The Eclipse of Excellence,* there is a powerful set of arguments for the tradition of grades and requirements. The point of view is not that of authority alone (which, for my part can't ever be a satisfactory *end*) but it is, on the contrary, based on the premise that all men are equal before an impartial system of evaluation: That idea has served the law and surely can serve the academy as well. Grading provides a still point in the turning world of thought. It gives both student and teacher a measure of accomplishment over time, while providing a common standard. Grades are not a measure of personality or moral worth; hence the argument that they are traumatic cannot prevail. And, of course, even if they were, is a little trauma such a bad thing? We cannot leave the womb without it.

Our regression toward the intellectually invertebrate is nowhere more clearly shown than in the matter of courses and requirements. "Relevance," for example, is much praised but rarely analyzed. It offers a short-term answer for problems which, like those of history or language, require a basis of memory and discipline. There is in fact a considerable logical problem to relevance. If we accept the idea that a curriculum should be immediately open to present concerns, then we accept also a chronology. For example, if courses are to be contemporary and crucial, then they ought to change their content in order to survey new problems each year. But if those problems are so vital, then they should really be taken up with even more immediacy and the focus of study changed each month. Correspondingly, a course that sincerely seeks true relevance can only gain by taking up events each week as they insistently develop. And, if they matter that much, changing issues should affect and change courses every day, hour and moment. In short, there is no finite end to relevance, so that a question of value is implied when we decide on the appropriate unit of time to consider it. And that question, involving a choice of alternatives, is of course the same issue with which we began.

Cause for Anxiety

[The American philosopher] Sidney Hook has written recently of the war against standards that it allows anything neither illegal nor hazardous. Course credit at one university has been allowed for candle making, conversation and love. According to the *Times*, one faculty member met his class under a table so that everyone could be on the same level. My own experience in foundation work has been less mordant. But I have been urged to support courses that would grade the feelings of students, which may be sincere but are certainly difficult to measure. That is especially true when the student gets pleasure from having learned nothing. And I have seen proposals to rewrite history not in order to rectify untruth but to create it. There have been proposals to give course credit for the ordinary business of life—which could be matched by the wish to give degrees for the same purpose. The problem is not that the human imagination is so comically various (for that we can be grateful), but that academic credit should be granted to 1 percent of the people for doing what the other 99 percent normally does. And of course, pastimes, devotions and ideologies, while probably interesting and entirely necessary, are not in themselves educational.

As we reflect on these things, we can see why so many teachers are more anxious now than ever before. It is not only that their authority is called into doubt (a reasonable man should be able to survive that), but that the courses they teach have lost conviction. Their colleagues too often are politically righteous and anti-intellectual; their students have no structure of tradition, rationale, grading or requirement to which they can relate. In addition to the external problems, there is the horrid example of capitulation on many campuses; academic freedom is simply forgotten if the teachers have the wrong views. Lacking their own conviction, without the security of academic freedom, uncertain even of that discourse and debate which were thought to be characteristic of the academy, they retire into themselves and become resigned to years of impotence. As if the university has come a thousand years through war and inquisition for that.

OLD MYTHS, NEW REALITIES [4]

Two million young Americans—and their families—this year will face The Great College Question. Where to go, *whether* to go, what to study, when to apply, how much it will all cost—such topics will consume vast amounts of time, energy, and emotion in households all over America.

Yet when the final decisions about colleges are made, many will be based not on logic and fact, but on ivy-covered misconception and myth. Probably no subject so basic to so many people is so widely misunderstood. And even if this were not so, college education, and its role in society, have changed so sharply in the past decade that new thinking may be required about the whole subject.

Here is a list of the most commonly held myths about higher education today. Following each are current facts

[4] From "Ten Common Myths About College." *Better Homes and Gardens.* 51:144+. My. '73. Reprinted from *Better Homes and Gardens* © Meredith Corp. 1973. All rights reserved.

that may help your prospective student formulate his important decisions.

1. It's hard to get into college.

This myth has probably caused more heartache and headache than any other. If it ever had a basis in fact, it does no longer. In the fall of 1972, colleges opened with space available for 300,000 additional students. New York University alone had five thousand fewer students enrolled than three years before. Eastern Oregon College even offered its students a cash bounty if they could recruit other applicants for the half-empty classrooms. And there will be even more space available in the future. The Carnegie Commission estimates that by 1980 there will be 280 more community colleges in operation—one within commuting distance of every college-age person in America.

Some colleges are still highly selective, of course. The elite schools, for example, may accept only one applicant in six. But even these schools have refocused their admissions policies to seek out more students from diverse backgrounds. One report states that any student who graduates in the upper 25 percent of his high school class will get into college somewhere—regardless of color, creed, sex, or size of his family income.

2. You must pass certain tests to get into college.

Most people assume that before enrolling in college, a student must pass a "College Board" or "SAT" test to determine whether he is "college material" and will be successful as an undergraduate. SAT and College Board scores used to be considered almost gospel by college admissions offices, but an increasing number have grown disenchanted with them.

Bowdoin College in Maine, for example, has dropped the use of SAT tests altogether, and officials there have been outspoken in urging that other colleges do the same. The chief reason: average SAT scores have been steadily dropping, yet students have better classroom records than ever. Some college officials feel that the tests, originally devised to rate applicants for elite Ivy League colleges in the 1930s, have little to do with the era of universal education in the 1970s. The tests also are said to be stacked against low-income and minority groups.

No test has been found yet which can predict accurately how well a student will do in college. A Brown University study, among others, showed absolutely no correlation between test scores and college grades. The best indicators of a student's college success are his high school grades and his class standing. But even these cannot identify the late-bloomer who suddenly "finds himself" in a college setting.

3. It's best to go to college right after high school.

Remember the GIs after World War II? Colleges now look back on them as the most dedicated and motivated students who ever appeared on American campuses. After a long interruption in their schooling, they came home with definite educational goals—and firm ideas about how to attain them. Far from being handicapped by the delay, many veterans breezed through the traditional four years of classes in three years or less.

Many colleges believe a large number of today's students would benefit if they too remained out of school a year, two years, or even longer to "get their heads together" and decide what they want to do. Such schools as William Smith and Hobart and Beloit College have instituted a policy of "deferred admission" for the high school graduate not quite ready to begin college and "leaves of absence" for students who want to pull out for a while.

Some experts have urged that such students be termed *stopouts* and not stigmatized as *dropouts*—and have even suggested that they be given college credit for job experience gained in the interim. These experts visualize stopping out as part of a system of lifetime education, in which students would alternate between work and study on a part- or full-time basis as their goals, needs, and situations changed over the years.

Meanwhile, many colleges have lifted the traditional time barriers for students who have established their career goals. The University of California is the latest institution to allow students to earn a degree in three years. One innovative New England institution has compressed the process even further: it combines the traditional four years of high school and four years of college into one solid, single six-year term.

4. Before you can go to college, you must finish high school.

A student can now enter college without ever setting foot in a high school, so long as he can pass a General Educational Development Test, a measure of what he has learned elsewhere. If he is attending high school, he may enter college as early as his junior year. Furthermore, if he is deficient in certain academic subjects, a college often will provide special remedial courses and even tutoring, especially if he is a minority student from an inadequate high school.

The trend is away from "proper" preparation. If a student thinks he knows enough about American history, he can take a test and if he passes, receive credit without ever attending class. The College Entrance Examination Board offers a degree credit College Level Examination Program (CLEP) for adults who are not formally enrolled in any college. Programs in New York, Massachusetts, and Pennsylvania allow a student to work for a degree without ever visiting a campus. He learns at home via television, correspondence, and self-study materials.

5. A good college education is very expensive.

If a student wants to attend Sarah Lawrence, it is. Or Yale, Stanford, Harvard, Pennsylvania, Oberlin, Vassar, Bennington, or any number of other elite private institutions around the country. Stanford, for example, has just increased tuition to $3,135 a year, and board and room costs to $1,425. A student who wants to study there thus can expect to lay out $5,000 a year—$20,000 for four years of education.

On the other hand, one of the most prestigious undergraduate institutions in the country charges students not a penny. The City College of New York admits residents tuition-free on a competitive basis. Community colleges in many states charge no tuition, or low tuition. Resident tuition in the California state colleges is only $164 a year. The State University of New York charges freshmen and sophomores $600, juniors and seniors $800. And today a student can cut his total bill further by earning college credit through high school Advanced Placement courses, by taking examinations for credit, or by studying through off-campus programs.

Also, a student who needs help can now spread the impact of his college bill over many years. State-guaranteed and federally insured student loans allow him to borrow up to $2,500 a year, to be paid back at low interest after graduation. Yale permits students to repay over a lifetime, the annual payment based on their yearly earnings. A Ford Foundation program spreads the payments over fifteen years and limits annual repayment to 6 percent of the student's income. And the most recent federal higher education act authorizes education grants of up to $1,400 per student per year. This figure, however, is reduced in relation to the expected family contribution, which is calculated by a formula based on family income.

6. A good college has many well-known professors.

Perhaps the oldest myth around is that one of the best ways to choose a college is to examine the credentials of the faculty. How many professors are Nobel prize-winners, or how many have published important books, or how many have served in key government posts?

As protesting students from Harvard to Berkeley have noisily pointed out, faculty "stars" often never appear in the undergraduate classroom. Their domain is the laboratory, the study, and the consulting office. Actual teaching of undergraduates often is left to teaching assistants and graduate students barely older than the undergraduates themselves. If the stars do any teaching at all, they often confine it to specialized classes at the graduate level.

Some institutions, such as Brown and Stanford, have tried to reverse this trend. Introductory freshman courses there are given by the prestigious members of the faculty. But in general stars concentrate on research, not teaching. Of course the best researchers are not necessarily the best teachers, anyway.

7. Private colleges are better than public colleges.

Many people believe that private institutions like the Ivy League and the Seven Sisters offer better education than that of public institutions and less famous schools.

Yet an American Council on Education rating of graduate school departments, ranked by scholars themselves, showed that many of the most highly regarded were in public universities, such as Wisconsin, Michigan, and California. The Berkeley campus of the University of California, for example, was one of the most highly ranked in many departments.

A tally of alumni in *Who's Who* a few years ago showed that Midwestern and Western institutions as a whole rated as high as the Eastern private colleges. Actually, no one has been able to prove that any given institution provides better education than any other given institution. Graduates of elite colleges may emerge with better academic records, more graduate school admissions, and better paying jobs, but this may be simply because they had better high school records—and more economic advantages—to begin with.

8. Small colleges are best because they always have smaller classes.

The belief in the great value of a tiny, friendly community of scholars living and working intimately together is one of the most treasured of myths. The informal atmosphere of a small school can be valuable—but there is such a thing as too small. The Carnegie Commission concluded that a liberal arts college with fewer than one thousand students could not offer the range of courses, the laboratory and library facilities, or the caliber of faculty for a first-rate education. A Stanford survey of sixteen thousand faculty across the country shows that teacher morale is at its lowest ebb in such small, financially starving educational institutions.

Great size, of course, has its own drawback. Students are reduced to numbers, identity vanishes, classes are conducted in huge auditoriums instead of in small classrooms or under a tree. So many different courses are offered that sometimes students are bewildered when told to choose among them.

Some colleges now offer the best of both. Michigan State University, for example, has its own network of small residential liberal arts colleges, each a separate entity but sharing common facilities and operating on the same campus. Neighboring small colleges have established consortia, under which they share laboratories, libraries, and even exchange faculty or hold joint classes in subjects for which single-campus demand is small.

9. *There are tremendous differences among colleges.*

The sad truth is that many colleges are very much alike. Although they now enroll more than eight million students from a wide range of backgrounds and wholly diverse needs, they differ—in the words of the Newman Task Force—largely in the degree to which they are trying to imitate Harvard. Regardless of size, location, or student body, they offer the same academic subjects taught almost exclusively by the lecture method.

The Newman Report blamed this sameness for the fact that about half the students who start college give up without getting a degree; they are bored to death with a curriculum and a teaching method that seem to have no application to their lives. Even religious colleges, which once used to have a distinctive identity, are becoming indistinguishable from their secular counterparts. One reason is that they must meet (along with secular colleges) certain standards of accreditation to qualify for government funds.

The best way to choose a college today is to (a) learn whether it offers the subjects the student is interested in; (b) visit the campus in person; and (c) talk to as many students and faculty as possible.

10. You need a college education to be successful.

That depends upon your definition of success. Some students, for example, actually lose money by going to college. They pay up to $5,000 a year for four years, meanwhile forgoing the wages they might have earned during that period, and then settle for a job paying no more than they might have obtained without a diploma. The Carnegie Commission on Higher Education estimated that perhaps 10 to 15 percent of students fall into this category—and should be dissuaded from entering in the first place.

The retrenchments of the 1970s have actually hit graduate degree holders harder than those with bachelor's degrees. One of the worries on many campuses is "the Ph.D. glut." The State University of New York has declared a moratorium on new doctoral programs, and Stanford and Yale have both cut back on the number of graduate students.

Meanwhile, business has shown less interest in hiring master's degree holders: they say the added education doesn't justify the added starting salary. Finally, the specialties which graduate students primarily pursue have been among those hardest hit economically. Cutbacks in government grants have reduced the need for scientists, and colleges are filled with faculty now that the baby boom years of the early fifties are over.

Yet college enrollment and faculty continue to grow each year, although the rate of growth is slower than in the

boom years of the 1960s. And, according to the United
States Office of Education, it generally *does* pay off in the
long run to hold a college degree. The average income for
four-year high school graduates is $9,566; for four-year
college graduates it's $14,158; and for five years of college,
or more, it's $16,276. And, of course, the self-employed
professionals—physicians, dentists, lawyers—can automatically count on a substantial income differential.

Moreover, whether or not a diploma pays off in dollars,
it is fast becoming essential in the world of work. A diploma
is a credential which many employers use to separate one
group of job-seekers from another, whether legitimately or
not. And many employers have upgraded job requirements
to call for a degree where none was needed in the past:
even the New York City police force wants its applicants to
have some college today.

Perhaps most important of all, education stretches the
mind, introduces the student to new thoughts and new interests, and prepares him to take a fuller role in society. And
education—whether it's gained in college or on one's own—
confers special intangible benefits in this era of increased
leisure time.

II. THE COST CRUNCH

EDITOR'S INTRODUCTION

Is college really worth the price, now ranging over $20,000 for four years in many institutions? We may instinctively shy from so crass a question with respect to something as sacred as education. But it may also be a healthy sign that more and more students are asking it. After all, American education has always been geared to practical, economic ends. If some faculty have dwelt in ivory towers, most students have had level-headed goals. Why shouldn't we gauge the value of higher education by utilitarian American standards?

The question becomes particularly acute in the face of rapidly rising tuition costs. As little as a decade ago, a good education could be had at outstanding state institutions for little more than $1,000 a year, room and board included. The price has more than doubled since and is still heading upward. If the recommendation made by the Committee for Economic Development is to be adopted, fees will go on rising by 10 to 12 percent a year for the next decade. The committee's main points are summarized in the first article in this section.

The cost squeeze raises questions not only about rising tuitions but about who shall pay them. Since state institutions now pay up to five sixths of the costs of every degree out of public funds, the taxpayer may be inclined to cry "Enough!" If the students themselves—or their parents—are to bear the burden, what of those who can barely afford the payments now? Shall they be subsidized by scholarships paid in part out of higher tuition fees from those who can afford them? Should they borrow against their futures?

This last question brings us full circle to the crass question posed at the outset. From a banker's viewpoint, the risks for such borrowing are clearly great, since two thirds of all college graduates earn no more money in their lifetimes than their counterparts with high school diplomas. Such odds should clearly discourage a realistic person.

These, then, are some of the dilemmas explored in this section. The first two articles outline the basic dimensions of the cost crunch confronting colleges and their students. The third indicates that the financial pinch extends to the sports arena, where a scramble for star athletes and the dollars they generate (and in some cases get) is also underway. The fourth article, from *Esquire*, makes a case against college as a wise financial investment, while the fifth, from *U.S. News & World Report*, indicates that on average it is probably worth it. The last article in this section provides a rational guide, for those who must decide who should and who should not go to college.

DIMENSIONS OF THE FINANCIAL CRISIS [1]

This policy statement was occasioned by the increasingly precarious financial condition and outlook of American colleges and universities. In 1971, about 60 percent of all private four-year colleges had actual deficits (i.e., expenditures exceeded incomes). At the same time, numerous major public institutions also incurred deficits. In 1972, the condition worsened. Most institutions have had to reduce their programs in order to correct or avoid deficits; some have disposed of parts of their campuses; others have closed.

When we inquired into the causes of the colleges' financial condition, we identified two closely linked major factors.

The topping-off of the boom in enrollment. In the 1960s, it was widely assumed that the opportunity for school-

[1] From "Introduction and Summary of Recommendations." Committee for Economic Development. *The Management and Financing of Colleges; a Statement by the Research and Policy Committee, October 1973.* Committee for Economic Development. 477 Madison Ave. New York 10022. '73. p 9-16. Reprinted by permission.

ing leading to the baccalaureate degree should be open to everyone who could pursue it successfully. This contributed to unparalleled enrollment increases as colleges and universities attempted, by expanding facilities and staffs, to accomplish what had been expected of them. The recent slackening in enrollments has now left many colleges with student vacancies and heavy fixed annual expenditures that are difficult or impossible to meet.

Rapidly rising costs exceeding the general rate of inflation. Between 1966 and 1969, the annual rate of increase in per student costs was 6 percent. Of this, an average of only 3.4 percent per year was due to general inflation. The present annual increase in per student costs, excluding inflation, is 3.3 percent. This is largely attributable to the lack of major productivity improvements in higher education. The labor-intensive character of education makes increases in productivity much more difficult to achieve in colleges and universities than in areas where mechanization and automation are possible. This situation is not uncommon in the service sector of the economy. Important improvements have occurred in higher education, especially in matters of quality; but here assessment of gains is difficult and sometimes impossible. Where productivity can be quantified, however, virtually no increases have occurred in recent decades.

Two major financial issues have emerged from these cost pressures. On the one hand, many private institutions are unable to raise tuition levels high enough to cover rising costs because of the competition from public institutions, many of which provide comparable schooling at lower prices and are often closer to the student's home. On the other hand, public institutions find it difficult or impossible to secure expanded or even constant appropriations from state legislatures, which face increasing demands on public funds for other purposes.

This describes briefly the central problem of colleges and universities today, namely, a serious and widening financial gap as increases in costs continue to outrun increases in revenues. Unless the financial trend is reversed, the nation will confront a decisive crisis in higher education: a lowering of the quality of education, the financial failure of needed institutions, and a loss of access to schooling for thousands of youths.

Colleges and universities often are not well equipped to cope with the economic forces that are now affecting them. This policy statement is an attempt to come to grips with the situation. We propose principles and modes of action in the management and financing of undergraduate education that we believe will encourage the survival of strong and effective institutions providing the high-quality education necessary to satisfy the needs of individuals and the nation. . . .

A Two-Part Strategy

Although a few institutions are now showing some improvement, many of our colleges and universities continue to be in financial trouble or are on the way to trouble. According to the Association of American Colleges, the number of private accredited four-year colleges and universities running current-fund deficits increased from about one third of all institutions in 1968 to nearly 60 percent by 1971. Furthermore, a study of the budget problem confronting forty-one private and public colleges and universities, made by the Carnegie Commission on Higher Education in 1971 and repeated in the spring of 1973, indicated that the situation has not shown any real signs of improvement. Of the eleven institutions that were "in financial difficulty" in 1971, six were better off two years later, two were in worse positions, and three reported no change. Of the eighteen "headed for financial trouble," half had improved, but the other half had slipped. The twelve institutions "not in financial trouble" also reported mixed results. Only one institution showed an improvement, six were in the same position, and five had slipped.

There have been steep cutbacks in cost among these forty-one institutions, mainly through holding down faculty salaries and cutting maintenance. Some of these costs cannot be deferred indefinitely. Corroborative data also indicate that in order to avert financial deficits many institutions have made significant retrenchments in programs. Such means of cost reduction may help temporarily to close the funding gap, but if colleges are to remain strong, there must be (1) increased income through higher tuition; (2) increased support from government; (3) larger gift income; (4) greater overall efficiency in the use of resources; (5) reduction in programs; or (6) some combination of these.

From our studies we conclude that colleges must take into account two fundamental conditions if they are to develop a realistic financial strategy for the 1970s.

First, because recent predictions of enrollment trends have proved most unreliable, we believe it is wiser, not to base policy on speculation about future trends, but rather to accept slower growth as a premise in planning. Planning should concentrate on consolidation, reorganization, and management improvement during a period of continued slowing of growth. It is always easier to cope with unexpected growth than with unanticipated declines. We do not, however, advise against the establishment of new community colleges where there is a clear need for an expansion of two-year instruction.

Second, we expect that in the decade ahead some additional resources may be obtained from government sources, and we assume that these increases will at least keep pace with increases in student enrollment and the cost of living. This means that we expect government support of higher education on a per student basis to remain more or less constant in real terms. Certainly, we do not anticipate the kind of large increases in governmental funding that occurred during the 1960s.

Although the future financial health of colleges depends

in part on increased revenues, it clearly requires a major dampening of the trend toward disproportionately increasing costs. Holding down costs is largely a problem of management of educational resources. In our view, improved management is the first part of an effective financial strategy for colleges. . . .

If productivity in the colleges does not increase at the same rate as in the economy generally, the amount needed to make up the difference will have to come from sources other than government. The student and his family constitute the only other major source of the funds available to pay for lagging productivity (i.e., cost increases per student in excess of those generated by inflation) and for quality improvement where improvement means increased costs. We believe that total private support through tuition and fees can be increased, assuming that government support is reallocated in ways that will make these increases less burdensome and more equitable.

SOARING TUITION [2]

Few people got excited when the Congress of 1862 passed Justin Morrill's bill giving the states parcels of federal land to endow new agricultural and mechanical colleges. The New York *Tribune,* summarizing the session's achievements, didn't consider it important enough to mention. Yet Morrill's land-grant bill—riding the tide of Jacksonian democracy, westward expansion and the agricultural and industrial revolutions—hurried along the development of a remarkable set of colleges and universities. In time, these institutions—places like the University of California or Missouri or North Carolina—became the social ladders on which the sons and daughters of the lower-middle class climbed into the professions. They took green farmboys and

[2] From "College Cost Squeeze: Tuition Controversy," by Larry Van Dyne, a writer for *The Chronicle of Higher Education. New Republic.* 169:11-13. D. 29, '73. Reprinted by permission of *The New Republic,* © 1973 The New Republic, Inc.

made them competent engineers, the sons of small merchants and trained them as lawyers, and eventually led women from housework into public school teaching. They did it by maintaining reasonably democratic admissions standards and low costs. As late as ten years ago a state resident paid only $304 a year in undergraduate tuition and fees at the University of California. At Missouri $215, and at North Carolina $279. The national average for institutions of their type was $280. Figuring in room and board, a year of education cost around $1000.

In the past decade, however, their tuition gradually rose as these institutions slapped together dormitories and classrooms to handle thousands of new students, hired more professors and increased their salaries, and tried to prove to the Ivy League that the colleges of the common man could be first class. By last fall [1973] tuition and fees were up to $638 at California, $540 at Missouri and $439 at North Carolina. Nationally the median charge was around $520 a year—still something of a bargain. That $520 covered only about a sixth of what a student's education actually cost; most of the rest came from state and federal revenues—in effect, the taxes paid by those upwardly mobile engineers, lawyers and schoolteachers. This has been the accepted way of financing public higher education.

This low-tuition policy is now being challenged. The debate over its wisdom is laid out in two influential study commission reports: *Higher Education: Who Pays? Who Benefits? Who Should Pay?* by the Carnegie Commission on Higher Education and *The Management and Financing of Colleges* by the business-dominated Committee for Economic Development (CED). Both urge a substantial boost in tuition at the public institutions. The Carnegie proposal envisions a less drastic rise than the CED's—about 10 to 12 percent a year over the next decade.

Stiff Reaction

The reaction has been swift and angry. The CED proposal is "extremely dangerous," says AFL-CIO President George Meany, and would "shatter the hopes of workers to insure that their children have the advantages of higher education." It reflects "the vested interest of a handful of wealthy businessmen whose families won't be affected," says the president of the National Student Association. "As long as I am chairman [of the House subcommittee that writes legislation on student aid]," says Representative James O'Hara (Democrat, Michigan), "I can assure the good people at the Carnegie Commission and the Committee for Economic Development that I am going to be very inhospitable to [such] proposals." Both of the Washington-based associations that look after the interests of the public institutions, the National Association of State Universities and Land-Grant Colleges (130 members) and the American Association of State Colleges and Universities [AASCU] (310 members), have rushed to defend low tuition.

To understand the arguments, we have to go back a bit and pick up a couple of the major shifts that have taken place since World War II.

For one thing the country's private institutions have begun to suffer financially; the very existence of some is threatened. Because they rely on tuition income to cover about 60 percent of their expenses, they have been forced —as costs have risen—to raise tuition. From the fall of 1964 to the fall of 1971 their average tuition nationally rose from $979 a year to $1776, and it's higher now. The gap between this rate and what the public institutions charge means that the private schools are at a big disadvantage in recruiting students. Faced with paying $2690 a year at Boston University or $520 at the University of Massachusetts, for instance, a parent may well wonder whether there's that much difference in quality or prestige, if any.

Many private institutions have empty seats in their class-rooms, and the declining birthrate alone suggests that their plight will get worse.

In the last couple of decades the public sector has become the dominant partner in the higher education enterprise. Public institutions enrolled just about half of all students in 1950; now they have three fourths. Public institutions—some of which have become more prestigious and higher quality than some of their private counterparts—now accommodate students from virtually all social classes, including the wealthy. At the University of Michigan, 12 percent of the freshmen in the fall of 1972 estimated that their families earned more than $40,000 a year; 43 percent put their parents in the over-$20,000 bracket. At the same time, despite recent gains by minorities, the children of families that earn less than $10,000 a year are still significantly underrepresented on college campuses. (The reasons of course, are only partly lack of money; going to college may have more to do with whether one was put in the college-prep "track" in high school.)

Given these trends the strategy of the Carnegie Commission and the CED is twofold: (1) Raise tuition; and (2) provide adequate federal scholarships for the poor. Beyond this general agreement there are important differences. Carnegie would raise charges until they cover about a third of the cost of instruction (compared to the current one sixth); CED wants them pegged at 50 percent of costs. Carnegie would string the increase out over ten years; CED would spread it over five in the four-year institutions and over ten years in the community colleges. The CED would keep the amount of tax money spent on higher education about the same as now, the extra dollars the colleges collect in tuition would be about all the new money that would be available for expanded student aid. Carnegie, on the other hand, would pour not only the extra tuition money into student aid, but additional millions in federal dollars as well.

The Carnegie report, which is the more detailed of the two, argues that its two-pronged policy would more equitably distribute the costs and benefits of higher education among the social classes than does the low-tuition device. The more affluent students (say those with family incomes of $15,000 a year or more) wouldn't be eligible for scholarships and would be forced to pay more nearly in line with their family capabilities. Poorer students (roughly those from families under $12,000 a year) would get scholarships. Students in the middle range ($12,000 to $15,000) would have to pay for their education out of savings or through loans. Part of the commission's case rests on the argument that many families can now afford higher tuition rates because their disposable incomes have (until very recently) been outstripping the rise in tuition.

Another major argument is that increased public tuition would help save the private colleges, which are viewed as an important source of diversity. If the private institutions keep their own tuition increases to about 6 percent a year, raising public tuition to one third of costs would narrow the troublesome "tuition gap" from the current 4 to 1 to about 2.5 to 1 by 1983. This new ratio, it is thought, would enable private institutions to compete for students more successfully.

Why Tuition Should Not Be Raised

The most formidable assault on this entire approach has come from the AASCU institutions, which are mostly ex-teachers' colleges with big middle-class clienteles. (Sixty percent of their students come from families that earn between $8000 and $20,000 a year.) Raising their rates would be vastly unfair to the middle class ($10,000 to $15,000 a year), they say, especially the lower end of the middle class. Higher tuition would mean that the well-to-do, who could get the money from home, would graduate debt free; the low-income could get scholarships and also graduate without the burden of debt, but middle-class students, unable to get either, would be forced to use up family savings (if any) or borrow heavily and spend their twenties paying back loans. That, the public institutions argue, is sticking it to the middle class.

It is also unfair, say the public institutions, to expect their students to pay higher rates to save the private sector. That amounts to taxing the six million students in public institutions to bail out colleges that enroll only two million. This makes about as much sense, says one president of a state university, "as forcing one person to undergo surgery because another person has appendicitis." It would be better to help the private institutions through direct institutional aid or through scholarships targeted for their students.

Another point raised by the public institutions is the possibility that both middle- and low-income students might get caught between the two prongs of the Carnegie-CED policy—tuition might go up, but student aid might not. Tuition rates and the funding of student-aid programs involve decisions by scores of people—officials of federal agencies like the Office of Management and Budget and the Office of Education, Congress, governors and state legislators, university trustees and administrators, voters in community college districts, and private bankers. The great danger, the public institutions believe, is that hard-pressed or fiscally conservative politicians might raise tuition and not use the revenue for student aid.

As an example of how student-aid funds are subject to shifting political and economic winds, one could cite the fate of the Basic Opportunity Grants program established by Congress in 1972 as part of a revised higher education act. The program authorized up to $1400 a year in aid for every student—minus whatever his family could be expected to contribute, given its income. But the appropriation level in the current year is so low that grants have been limited to freshmen and average only about $260.

THE SCRAMBLE FOR ATHLETES [3]

America's college campuses, rocked by unrest in the 1960s, are being shaken today by a new crisis: a frenzied "slave market" in recruiting and paying athletes. Many educators warn that the crisis is approaching a public scandal, and they attribute it to a national mania to "win at any cost."

But the cost is spreading far beyond the 50,000 athletes and coaches who are staging 32,000 basketball and 3,000 football games this year, or the hundreds of millions of dollars the games will generate. The cost, they say, is being paid in the growing corruption of high school students, in a distortion of the role of sports in education, and in the moral climate surrounding the schools. Even successful coaches like Frank Broyles of Arkansas have predicted that "if something isn't done, the lid is going to blow off."

"It's the worst I've seen in my twenty-three years of coaching," said Joe Paterno, whose football team earned $500,000 for Penn State in the Orange Bowl . . .[in the winter of 1973–1974].

Behind the frenzied recruiting and "win at any cost" mania is a rising tide of red ink. Though sports attendance and revenue at a majority of the nation's 1,120 four-year "team" colleges are at record levels, nine of every ten college athletic departments are running in the red. The chief reason: costs have doubled in the last decade, in some places in the last five years.

Athletic budgets of $2 million or $3 million are not unusual at major colleges. At a few of the superpowers such as Ohio State, they have reached the $4 million mark. When Louisiana State's football team went to the Orange Bowl last New Year's Day, air fares for the band alone cost $25,000. UCLA budgets $500,000 for athletic scholarships. Harvard,

[3] From "Sports Recruiting: A College Crisis." *Reader's Digest*. 105:107-112. Jl. '74. Copyright © 1974 by The New York Times Company. Reprinted by permission, as condensed in the July 1974 *Reader's Digest*.

which offers no athletic scholarships and prohibits its coaches from making recruiting trips, spends $12,000 a year on adhesive tape. Four colleges have dropped football during the last year, 40 over the last ten years, because the pressure grew too great.

Win—or Collapse

Count as a major factor the frenzy of the American public. For millions, intercollegiate athletics are a way of life: an exciting, entertaining, often ego-building source of pride for alumni, townspeople, television viewers, state legislators, even students. On home-game days at the University of Nebraska, the stadium, which seats 76,000, becomes the third-largest community in the state. In some areas, university officials feel that legislatures are more disposed to send money down to State U if the team is winning. Says Richard Moll, director of admissions at Bowdoin College in Maine, "Winning in some visible sport may charm alumni to give money. This is a policy handed down to my office."

Can one wonder, then, at the steepening of the competition for athletes who may thrust a college into the national spotlight, the television picture, the post-season bowl games—or just into the black?

Recruiting is worse now than it used to be because the recruited athlete today isn't just protecting the coach's job [observes Don Canham, athletic director at the University of Michigan, whose budget runs to $3.5 million a year]. He's supporting the whole program. So there's more pressure than ever before on the recruiter to con the kid. Now if he doesn't win, the whole thing collapses, as it has at some schools.

Coach and athlete operate at one end of the chase; at the other, supplying the pressure, are college presidents trying to build stadiums or libraries, alumni trying to build the prestige of alma mater, and state officials trying to build a record with the public. "I'd like to get rid of sports recruiting and big-time football," the president of a Southwest Conference college confessed recently. "If I did, though, I couldn't stay in this state for two days."

In their rush for the teen-age talent, universities are increasingly ignoring or sidestepping the recruiting-code rules of the National Collegiate Athletic Association [NCAA]. The chief rule says that a college may provide tuition and fees, room, board, books and $15 a month for incidental expenses. Violations include payments to high-school stars, tampering with their grades, forging their transcripts, finding substitutes to take their exams, promising jobs to their parents and buying them cars.

"I had offers of everything from girls to wardrobes to freezers stocked with food," recalls fullback Matt Snell, who chose Ohio State and then set many of the New York Jets' rushing records. Varsity football regulars at Ohio State received a batch of season tickets, Snell says, "and if you were a pretty good player you could get an alumnus to take a ticket off your hands for $300."

About twenty universities are publicly censured each year, and an undisclosed number are warned privately. Oklahoma has been placed on probation three times in the last 17 years in football; Southwestern Louisiana, twice in 6 years during a sudden rise to prominence in basketball. Cornell was already on probation in hockey last winter when it admitted violations in basketball. In January [1974], the NCAA penalized Long Beach State because of evidence that, among other things, automobiles had been purchased for athletes and money had been supplied them.

They just don't give automobiles [says NCAA investigator Warren S. Brown]. They backstop themselves some way. We've had instances where, on the bank records of loan papers, it's the young man or his parent—but we've proved that they got the cash to make the payments. That's the same as giving him a car.

Some kids get "letters of interest" from colleges while they are still in the ninth grade. Rick Mount, now in the American Basketball Association, started getting letters in the eighth grade. Last year [1973], Butch Lee, a high-school-senior basketball star in New York City, got letters of this sort from more than two hundred colleges. The rush is even reaching into sports that do not fill stadiums, like swimming, lacrosse, wrestling and women's basketball, as well as into sideshows that do not even qualify as sports, like rodeo and baton-twirling.

Wooing the Winners

About one hundred schools wrote to Sandy Mayer, who was a Long Island, New York, high school tennis star at the time, extolling their tennis program. One was Rice University. Even now, several years later, Mayer fondly recalls his weekend at Rice. "As soon as I got off the plane, they talked a guy into moving out of his apartment, and I got the nicest rooms on campus."

That evening, Mayer went to a basketball game, and one of the tennis-team members motioned to a small group of coeds and asked, "Which one would you take if you had your choice?" Mayer picked the prettiest one and was told, "She's yours."

Mayer fell for the girl. Even though he had always believed he wanted to go to Stanford, he wavered because of the coed. "I felt a lot of pressure in making the decision," he says. "I was trying hard not to be swayed by that girl." (Mayer finally chose Stanford.)

Steve Spurrier, now quarterback with the San Francisco 49ers, visited 12 of the 50 colleges that invited him. He heard recruiters tell him a dozen times, "You're the type of kid I'd want my daughter to marry." At Vanderbilt, he flew up in the governor's private helicopter to Nashville, then visited in the governor's mansion where "we shot some pool."

Of all the big college-football days, few are more highly dramatized than the second Saturday in December in the Deep South. It is Signing Day, when more than 150 of the South's strongest, quickest schoolboys sign college-football agreements with ten Southeastern Conference teams, or with a half dozen southern independents.

More than 150 football coaches, team trainers and full-time recruiters station themselves in towns across the South, usually a day in advance. Many have alumni-donated planes and pilots. "If you don't fly," one coach remarks, "you die." Alabama, one of the most effective recruiting universities in the nation, had 10 recruiters stationed in 6 states last December. They used 2 airplanes—owned by the university.

It is something like a wedding day. Mothers bake cakes and dress up. Family doctors, high school coaches, preachers, relatives and neighbors are invited for living-room ceremonies. There is handshaking, backslapping, prayer. By mid-afternoon, telephone lines at university athletic offices are tied up by fans and newsmen seeking signees' names and vital statistics. Newspapers in seven states carry complete signing lists on Sunday morning, with heights, weights, hometowns and credentials, and often with pictures and family interviews.

Increasingly, the search for blue-chip gladiators to balance the athletic-department budget has led to black communities. However, concerned leaders are beginning to question the morality of young athletes being systematically enticed by college, high school and even junior-high recruiters. Growing numbers of critics see the recruiting game as a swindle that plunders the black community and leaves thousands of untrained, uneducated victims on the athletic slag heap.

"A kid can't even read, they'll let him play high school basketball," says Myles Dorch, a former basketball recruit who got the college education he wanted and who now tries to teach heavily recruited young athletes how to avoid academic bankruptcy. "The coaches don't give a damn," he continues, "and neither do the schools. No guidance. No relationship except three to five in the gym, and games. 'Don't worry about going to class—we'll fix you up.' Just pad their grades, and push 'em right on out."

The corruption, claims Dorch, carries over into the college scene: "I know of five kids right now in top-ranked colleges playing basketball who didn't graduate from high school." Only 62 percent of the nation's basketball professionals playing last winter had their college degrees. Only two players on the twelve-man Kansas City-Omaha Kings roster during the 1973–74 season received their degrees.

For those who make the pros, that may be all right. But the odds against a boy's making the pros are astronomical. For every Walt Frazier of the New York Knicks, with his $30,000 Rolls-Royce, thousands are rejected. Of the 5,700 seniors playing basketball in America's colleges last year, only 285 were drafted by the pros, and only 100 signed.

"It's an exploitation, a rip-off," says Roscoe C. Brown, Jr., director of New York University's Institute of Afro-American Affairs. "The boys are deluded and seduced by the athletic fleshpeddlers, used for public amusement, and discarded—most of them without the skills needed for servicing or enriching the community."

What Price Victory?

The 670 colleges in the NCAA are policed by only five investigators, led by Warren Brown. Recently, the University of Texas called for NCAA funds to beef up enforcement, and even volunteered $5000 to start things rolling. Other officials, including the Rev. Edmund P. Joyce, executive vice president of Notre Dame, have said that they would contribute to such a fund. But at its convention . . . [in 1973], the NCAA decided against any addition to Brown's staff.

Still, on hundreds of college campuses, the day of reckoning appears to be drawing near. Beneath the roar of the crowds, educators, administrators and even a few coaches are finally beginning to ask: "What price victory?"

One critique of the situation was voted . . . by the National Association of Basketball Coaches, after a wave of protests from the coaches themselves. Another has been started by the American Council on Education, with financial help from the Ford Foundation and the Carnegie Corporation, and with some prompting from the Association of American Universities. Its task force has completed a six-month pilot study and urges a full-scale study of the problem. "We've got to slow down this drive on campuses to be 'No. 1,'" says George Hanford, executive vice president of the College Entrance Examination Board and head of the task force. "Something needs to be done to break the cycle."

Hanford's comments on recruiting abuses are restrained—partly, some of his colleagues feel, because he wants to avoid antagonizing the sports establishment. Privately, several members of the task force call recruiting and subsidization "more insidious" today than ever.

If Hanford and his colleagues can get a go-ahead for their full-scale study, it will be the first major independent appraisal of college athletics since a Carnegie Foundation for the Advancement of Teaching Report in 1929. That report stirred nationwide furor. It found the college-sports establishment "sodden" with commercialism and professionalism. It called for an end to the costly "spectacles" and a return to broader student participation in low-key intramural athletics. And it raised two basic questions about the role of organized athletics in American college life:

"What relation has this astonishing athletic display to the work of an intellectual agency like a university?"

"How do students, devoted to study, find either the time or the money to stage so costly a performance?"

In the deepening campus crisis of 1974, students and educators . . . [were] asking those same questions again.

IS IT WORTH THE PRICE? [4]

This is the story of a mythical boy we'll call Joe, whose grades were so good that his high school guidance counselor got him to apply to Princeton as well as his hometown state school.

Both colleges accepted Joe, but he didn't know what he wanted to do. Sometimes he thought it might not be too

[4] From "College: Dumbest Investment of All," by Caroline Bird and Stephen G. Necel. Caroline Bird is the author of *The Case Against College* (McKay, 1975). *Esquire.* 82:102+. S. '74. Reprinted by permission of Caroline Bird. First published in *Esquire* magazine.

bad to hang around working at the garage for a while, sorting out his mind.

"Princeton's expensive," said Joe. "It says here that tuition, room, board, and personal expenses cost $5,730. That allows $650 for personal expenses, including books and travel to get there, but I bet everyone spends more. It's full of rich boys. You know we don't have that kind of money."

"Maybe not for Princeton," said his mother. "But you could swing it if you went to State. You could work at the garage part-time and live at home."

Joe didn't mind the garage, but he didn't much like the idea of living at home. It all sounded like just so much more high school. Princeton offered him a lot of financial aid, but mostly loans and campus jobs he wasn't sure he'd like. Was a Princeton education worth the hassle?

"Son, you're a fool not to go to college," Joe's father said. "It says right here that you will have earned $199,000 more by the time you're sixty-four if you go to college instead of getting a job out of high school and working all your life the way I've done. And if you don't go now, while you have the chance, you'll never go."

Joe nodded, but he wasn't convinced, and his parents didn't push the subject. "After all, it's his life," they told each other.

The morning of his high-school graduation, a telegram arrived for Joe. It read:

YOUR GRADUATION PRESENT IS TOTAL COST OF ANY COLLEGE YOU CHOOSE FOR FOUR YEARS TO SPEND ANY WAY YOU PLEASE STOP CERTIFIED CHECK FOLLOWS ADVISE OF REQUIRED CAPITAL SUM CONGRATULATIONS   UNCLE SAMUEL

"I don't give a damn *what* you do with the money, young man," Uncle Sam cackled when they phoned him. "All I want is a letter explaining why you are doing it."

The first job was to let Uncle Samuel know how much he was in for—before he changed his mind. This proved less of a problem than they had feared. Princeton itself publishes a suggested budget—with higher tuition costs almost every year. Joe and his parents figured that tuition, room and board, and personal expenses for Joe's four years would come to $22,256.

It sounded like a lot of money. "I've never had $22,256 in one piece at any time in my whole life," Joe's father said.

"I guess it's too much to blow," Joe said, regretfully. He was thinking about Europe for the summer.

Joe's mother was thinking along the same lines. "If your father and I had ever had $22,256 at your age," she said rather sternly, "we would have put it right in the savings bank so we'd have enough in there by now to send you to Princeton and go to Europe ourselves."

Joe's father was good at arithmetic. He had just bought a little pocket calculator and was itching for a chance to use it. "I'm forty-eight now. If I had been able to put $22,256 by at today's interest rate of 7.5 percent when I was Joe's age, we'd have $217,663 in the bank right now instead of a bunch of bills." He whirred a little longer. "And at sixty-four, I'd have $735,171 in the bank!"

"More than twice as much as you said a college graduate stands to gain over his lifetime in extra earnings!" Joe's mother exclaimed.

Joe's father shook his head. "No. It's not a fair comparison. The return on $22,256 in the savings bank is interest, and you are leaving it in the bank to compound. The return on $22,256 invested in a college education is extra income, and you're letting the college graduate eat it up every year."

Joe's mother was getting a little confused. "All right, but then which way is better? Should Joe put the money in college, or should he put it in the bank?"

Uncle Samuel's nephew had been doing a little figuring of his own. "If I go to Princeton, I have to live on the budget Princeton says you can get by on, because that's what Uncle Samuel will give me. If I go to work in the garage, I'll be making good money. I will be able to live better than a college student."

"So what?" asked his mother.

"Uncle Samuel said he'd put up the *total* cost of college," Joe continued. "I say that the total cost includes the money I would have earned if I had continued working at the garage all through the four years instead of during the summers only."

"Well I hope you don't ever say a thing like that to your Uncle Samuel!" Joe's mother exploded. "Talk about ingratitude! And you aren't even logical. You sound like the woman who tried to convince her husband she was putting money in the bank every time she didn't buy a hat!"

Getting Professional Advice

Joe and his father took the argument straight to the Princeton economics department. The economics department had heard about Uncle Samuel's offer and they sided with Joe. There was nothing fishy about forgone income, they assured Joe and his father. Economists count it all the time.

Sometimes Joe's father saw it and then at other times he didn't see it, but since he had only a high school education, he didn't like to argue with Princeton professors. Joe's mother wasn't convinced at all. She was sure the professors were in cahoots to whop up the amount of that certified check.

"And another thing," she went on. "You can't count the room and board at Princeton and those forgone earnings too, because if you *had* earned them, you would have paid your room and board *out* of them."

Joe conceded the point. After deducting the room, board, and personal expenses exclusive of books and travel to Princeton Junction, the forgone wages dwindled from $20,000 to $11,925. That sounded reasonable, but they still couldn't figure what to do with the forgone wages or how to use them to decide whether Joe would be better off investing in college or investing in the bank. Joe's mother was dead set against any way of reckoning that asked Uncle Samuel to pay the forgone income.

"If Uncle Samuel gives you $22,256, and you use that money to go to Princeton, it will all be gone in four years," his mother figured, out loud. "You'll have a nice, shiny Princeton diploma and no money in the bank. If instead you take the $22,256, put it in the savings bank, and go to work at the garage, you can pay me what Princeton says you need for room and board and put the $11,925 you have left over in the bank."

"And if he adds that $11,925 to his original nest egg as he earns it," Joe's father announced, calculator in hand, "he'll have $43,578 when he is twenty-two instead of a Princeton diploma."

Is there anything a penniless twenty-two-year-old can do with a bachelor's degree that will ever put him ahead of a twenty-two-year-old who has $43,578 in the bank instead? They decided to ask their friendly local banker.

The question stumped him, but he tried not to let on. "I wouldn't say that investing a capital sum in college is what you would call a safe investment," he said. "If you get run over by a truck, all that knowledge is lost to your heirs. And here's another thing. You're counting, for your return, on earning more money because of your diploma. Well, maybe you will and maybe you won't. Almost a third of college graduates don't earn more, on the average, than high school graduates."

He sized Joe up with a long, friendly look.

Joe squirmed. He was thinking about having all that money tied up in his head. He was wondering whether his head was the sort that would make it pay.

"A lot of success is really luck," the banker continued, not unkindly. "College may add something to the ability you brought with you to it. You might meet someone who would put you onto a good job. But I happen to think that college men earn more because they are brighter or better off to begin with; a lot of them would earn just as much if they didn't go. If I'm right—and smart people like Christopher Jencks, the Harvard educator, and Fritz Machlup, the Princeton economist, agree with me—then getting accepted at Princeton has already marked you for financial success. And if that's true, may I suggest, as your friendly local banker, that you deposit that certified check with us as soon as it arrives?"

Joe didn't like that idea at all, and the unexpected pitch jolted him into sarcasm. "And I suppose that if I add the $11,925 I can save over the next four years by living like a college student, and never spend any of it, I'll be a millionaire when I retire from the garage at sixty-four?"

"I think we could arrange that for you," the banker said almost unctuously. "If you'll excuse me just a moment, I'll run the calculations out on our computer."

Computers are fearsomely fast. "Just as I thought," he announced happily, as he returned bearing a few folds of computer paper. "If you deposit your $22,256 now at today's savings-bank interest rate of 7.5 percent compounded daily, and add the $11,925 as it is earned, you will have precisely $1,062,106 at age sixty-four."

"And if I invest that money in my head and bank the extra earnings I stand to make every year as it is earned?"

"You'd have $1,222,965," supplied the banker. "I thought you'd want to know so I ran it out for you from 1972 Census figures on income by age and education. Of course, income taxes would shrink both capital sums."

Joe lost all patience. "I don't care about a few hundred thousand dollars one way or another, or a million dollars either, if I'm not going to see any of it until I'm sixty-four. I want to know how much I'll have to spend in the next few years."

"Okay," said the friendly banker. "Let's see what happens if you spend all the returns from your investment in college and all the returns from the $43,578 you'll have in the bank if you go to work in the garage instead. The first year you're out of college, your diploma will earn you $96 more than you would make at the garage, nowhere near as much as the $3,226 interest would draw down if you invested in the savings bank. Your second year out, college would net you $558 for riotous living compared with the $3,226 interest from the savings bank. The extra income college gets you won't catch up with the savings-bank interest on the money college has cost you until you are thirty-one, and the *peak* payoff of college doesn't come until you are fifty-three, when earnings are $7,059 more. After that, the advantage declines until it's $5,833 for sixty-four-year-olds."

"What do you think the outlook will be by then?" Joe's father asked.

"I haven't a clue," said the banker. "Inflation may increase everyone's dollar earnings, but an oversupply of college graduates could narrow the advantage they have in income, too. The fifty-three-year-olds who were earning $7,059 more for college when the Census took its reading in 1972 were twenty-two-year-olds in 1941 when a diploma was something exceptional in the job market."

Balancing Risks

Joe's father was trying to sort it all out in his head. "One way he gets a steady income in dollars for forty-two years. The other way, he gets a bigger income much later in life. Isn't there any way to compare the two investments?"

"Of course there is," the banker answered. "You know that merchants give you a discount for paying now instead of later. Well, you can discount any future sum the same way. Discounted at 7 percent, which is conservative the way interest rates are going, the extra earnings of college men are worth $49,877, while the uncompounded interest—the annual $3,226 you were so eager to spend—plus discount on the capital sum you'd have left at the end—come down to a net present value of $48,825. Remarkably close, isn't it?"

"What do you think Joe should do?" his mother asked.

"*Dollarwise*, Princeton is the worst investment Joe could make," the banker answered. "The considerable risk of carrying his capital around inside his head will return him, in extra income, little more than we'll pay him for keeping his money at absolutely no risk in a savings account. To figure it another way, the internal rate of return on his Princeton education works out to 9.5 percent. We figure that a minimum-risk investment has to return at least 10 percent— and college is not a minimum-risk investment. It's so risky, as a matter of fact, that we won't lend students the cost of their tuition unless the Government guarantees the risk."

"What's your idea of a better investment?" Joe's father wanted to know.

"It pains me to say so—I'd love to have that money in our bank—but he could lock it all in at today's high interest rates for long-term corporate bonds yielding from 8.5 to 13 percent. If he expects to earn enough money to worry seriously about taxes, he could put it in tax-free municipals which can carry interest as high as 7.5 percent. Or he could put it in an investment trust, where a money manager could move it from the stock market to Treasury bills and other high-interest-bearing money-market instruments. . . . Some of those managed by banks have yielded 8 percent and the return could easily be more. . . ."

This was all too abstract for Joe's mother. "But what do you personally think Joe should do?"

"That depends on Joe," said the banker warily. "He says he likes cars. If he went to work in the garage, and banked Uncle Samuel's money, he'd have $68,766 in the savings bank at the ripe old age of twenty-eight. Enough to buy out the garage after he's learned the business. Or he could buy a franchise—Dairy Queen, McDonald's, Carrols— with less risk than he runs of returning his investment in Princeton. Or he could buy a liquor store."

"That would bore me to death," Joe put in.

"Maybe," said the banker. "But dollarwise, we're talking about twice as big a return as college will give you."

"Thank you," said Joe. "I'll think it over."

Joe went home. He thought it all over. He drafted many

long letters to Uncle Samuel and tore them up. The letter
he sent was short and noncommittal:

Dear Uncle Samuel,
    Mother and father and I want to thank you for your generous
offer, and since you said I could do anything I want with it—
however foolish—I am going to blow it all on Princeton.
    All the other alternatives would bring me more money, but
after exploring them, I don't think I'd like them. The truth is,
Uncle Samuel, I just don't feel like committing myself to anything
right now, and Princeton sounds like a pleasant place to be for
the next four years.

Gratefully,
Joe Blow

P.S. Money isn't everything.

ON THE AVERAGE, IT'S WORTH IT [5]

Reprinted from *U.S. News & World Report*.

Now given added emphasis in a new study is the hard
dollars-and-cents value of education as reflected in the incomes of men with various levels of schooling.

In a report from the Bureau of the Census, these were
major findings:

☐ Men who have completed college have average annual
earnings from two to three times higher than men with only
grade-school education.

☐ Over a lifetime, men with some level of postgraduate
work—five years or more of college—will earn an average of
more than $800,000, compared with less than $300,000 for
those who have fewer than eight years of schooling....

The Census study covered only male workers and did
not include such income as capital gains. The fact that more
years of education means, on the average, a higher income
is not a new phenomenon. But the Census study pointed up
some fast-moving changes in educational and income levels.

    [5] From "College Grads vs. Others: Earnings More Than Double." *U.S. News
& World Report*. 77:42. Jl. 22, '74.

In the words of the study, the latest in the "Current Population Reports":

"The educational attainment of the male population in the United States has increased considerably during the past sixteen years. In March 1973 the median years of school completed by men twenty-five years old and over was 12.3 years, or about the equivalent of a high school education, whereas in March 1957, it was 10.4 years.

"Between March 1957 and March 1973 the proportion of males who terminated their schooling after four years of high school increased by about two fifths and the proportion of males completing four or more years of college rose by two thirds.

"As can be expected, there was a reduction in the proportion of men who terminated their schooling with elementary school, dropping from about 19 percent in March 1957 to roughly 12 percent in March 1973."

The report noted that, although a high ratio of men end education with a high school diploma, "there has been an upward trend in the proportion of males completing their schooling beyond high school." The figures:

"In March 1959 about 8 percent of the 46.3 million males twenty-five years old and over had completed one to three years of college and in March 1973 about 12 percent of the 53.1 million males had attained this level of schooling—a gain of 48 percent.

"Between March 1959 and March 1973 men completing their formal education with a bachelor's degree rose from 6 percent to 9 percent. A relative gain was registered by men with postgraduate studies completed. Men completing five or more years of college rose from 4 percent in March 1959 to 7 percent in March 1973."

The Census study found that, "in step with the rise in the educational attainment level of the male population," there had also been significant changes in mean incomes over the past sixteen years. Measured in constant 1972 dollars, the mean income of all men twenty-five years and older increased in that span by 49 percent.

The study concluded:

"An important factor in this increase is that more and more males are continuing their schooling which in turn provides the opportunity to enter into skilled occupations yielding higher income returns."

Between 1956 and 1972—measured in constant dollars—mean lifetime incomes of all men from age eighteen to death rose from $322,000 to $471,000, up 46 percent.

Broken down by educational levels, the gains in lifetime earnings over the 1956-1972 period were:

    Elementary—$275,000 to $344,000
    High school—$376,000 to $480,000
    College—$573,000 to $758,000

WHO SHOULD GO TO COLLEGE? [6]

Many of the students now in college have no sound reason for being there, and would not have entered if they had been given valid information. They are not motivated by the vocational goals of higher education because they have not decided what kind of work they want to do. They are not ready for further liberal education because, after 12 years of elementary and secondary schooling, they are fed up with schooling. They want to escape from the academic environment and move out into the world, but high school counselors and parents—believing deeply, as Americans always have, in the value of education—have urged them into college.

No other nation in the history of the world has ever provided higher education for so large a percentage of its youth.

[6] From article by Paul Woodring, Distinguished Service Professor at Western Washington State College. *Education Digest.* 38:12-15. Mr. '73. Condensed from *Who Should Go to College.* Phi Delta Kappa Educational Foundation. P.O. Box 789. Bloomington, Ind. 47401. '72. p 7-11, 35-8. Reprinted by permission.

Nearly 80 percent of our young people today graduate from high school, and well over half of these enter a college of some kind. But attrition rates in our colleges are much higher than in Europe. In England, only 14 percent of the young people enter universities, but 87 percent of these complete the work for a degree. Here, where the percentage entering is three or four times as high, fewer than half receive their baccalaureate degrees four years later. Some, of course, are in two-year terminal courses, and some receive degrees later.

Eric Ashby, a noted English educator who has made a careful study of our colleges, attributes this high attrition rate to our "liberal and diverse admission standards."

It is a part of the privilege of an affluent society to be able to sample things and reject them [he has written]. But the American society may not be affluent enough to allow this privilege in higher education in the 1980s. It may then become unrealistic politically, too, to spend millions of dollars on places in college occupied by persons who are not gifted enough, or do not have the motivation, to benefit from the education which college provides.

The cost of providing space and instruction for the millions of young Americans who enter college and then leave without degrees runs into billions of dollars annually. As a nation, we must decide whether this is the best possible use of the money available for higher education.

There are about 2,600 colleges in the nation, of which more than 1,600 are four-year, degree-granting institutions. Only a minority of these turn away qualified applicants. During the 1960s, many students and their parents were led to believe that it was almost impossible to enter college without exceptionally high test scores and high school grades, but the fact is that it was never really difficult for a student to find a college that would accept him if he were willing to search. Many of the publicly supported colleges, when faced with larger numbers, simply expand their facilities and enlarge their faculties. And many of the less well known church-related colleges have great difficulty in attracting enough students to fill their dormitories and classrooms.

The percentage of high school graduates choosing to enter college is no longer growing nearly as rapidly as it did in the sixties, and in some parts of the nation has declined. By the late seventies and early eighties, when the declining birthrate begins to affect enrollments, many colleges will be trying hard to attract more students. The prospects for the next two decades are that, while it will still be somewhat difficult to get into some of the more famous institutions, it will not be at all difficult to get into college.

Yet the question remains: How many can profit from higher learning?

Appropriate for All?

Equality of educational opportunity has always been an American goal. Most persons agree that access to institutions of higher education ought not to be denied to anyone on the basis of sex, race, religion, social class, or even lack of money. There is much less agreement as to whether admission to college should be restricted on the basis of intellectual capacity as measured by entrance test scores, high school grades, or other yardsticks of academic potential. Though a few educators contend that colleges should be open to all, regardless of intellectual capacity, the majority believe that there is a minimal intellectual level below which any education properly called "higher" is an impossibility, and that such education, by its very nature, cannot be made appropriate for all.

Professor Fritz Machlup of Princeton said recently, "Higher education is far too high for the average intelligence, much too high for the average interest, and vastly too high for the average patience and perseverance of the people here and anywhere." This conviction is reflected in the admission standards of those more highly selective colleges and universities whose students are from the upper 5 percent, or even 2 percent, of high school graduating classes. However, many colleges, private as well as public, have for many years admitted a much higher percentage, including many who did not take "college preparatory" courses in high school. And some of the students who would have been denied admission to the prestigious colleges have gone on to graduate and professional schools, and have made significant contributions to the world as statesmen, scholars, and members of the learned professions.

In light of such facts, the view that higher education is appropriate for only a select few—and that the present entrance requirements are valid for identifying that few—is indefensible. It does not follow, however, that higher education is appropriate for everyone. As traditionally defined, it clearly is not appropriate for those who, even after preparatory courses, cannot read difficult books with understanding, who cannot express themselves in speech and writing, or who are bewildered by scientific theories and mathematical symbols. Whether colleges should alter their programs in such a way as to make them less intellectually demanding, and hence appropriate for a larger number of young people, is one of the problems that must be faced.

Need Accurate Information

Because any high school graduate can find some college that will accept him, the decision to go to college or not to go will be made by students themselves, with more or less prodding from their parents. Consequently, it is essential that they be given accurate information on which to base the decision.

Much of the information now being disseminated is inaccurate, misleading, and erroneously interpreted. Many students have been led to believe that it is difficult to find a job without a college education, when in fact about 80 percent of the jobs in the nation do not require such education. They have been led to believe that degrees are essential for financial success, when the fact is that 68 percent of the adults now in the upper-income brackets have reached that position without college degrees. They have been led to expect that a degree will confer more social status than it does today or is likely to in the future. On the other hand, they have not been made adequately aware of the true non-vocational, nonfinancial values of liberal education.

If more accurate information were provided, many would still enroll in liberal arts colleges because they really want a liberal education; others would enroll as a first step toward a professional career. A larger number would choose short vocational courses in community colleges or trade schools. But a substantial number would wisely decide not to enroll in any college immediately after high school graduation. They would gain a maturing experience by leaving home after high school graduation, looking for jobs whereby to support themselves, and meeting the responsibilities of adult life head on. This is a better solution for reluctant students than college, where they would likely become troublesome to the college and a disappointment to their parents. When counselors and parents urge such students to go to college, they are giving bad advice because higher education cannot be forced on anyone, no matter how high his IQ, if he lacks motivation. No student is ready for liberal education at the college level unless he wants it. He must enjoy reading and putting his thoughts on paper. He must have intellectual curiosity and be eager to continue learning. He must want to know, to think, and to understand.

Late Entry

Some of those who decide against college at eighteen will find satisfying employment and move ahead without further formal education, but many will develop a real desire for it at some later date. For this reason, institutions of higher education should be open to all adults, whether they decide to enter at twenty-one, thirty, or later. Because many of the older students will have family responsibilities that make full-time attendance difficult, opportunities for college work, both liberal and vocational, could be made available in all communities on a part-time basis. The teachers should include some of the best professors, selected for their special qualifications for working with mature students. Liberal credit examination should be available for those who have learned outside of school the equivalent of what is learned in college. And the states should provide the same kind of support for colleges enrolling older students that they provide for conventional colleges.

Many of those who enter college later in life become much better students than if they had been sent to college by their parents at eighteen, as the experiences of vetrans who attended college under the GI Bill gave clear evidence.

When continuing education on a part-time basis is upgraded and made available in all parts of the nation, there will be no good reason for urging every boy and girl to go to college immediately after high school graduation. Many will be able to make a wiser decision later.

Increasingly, eighteen-year-olds are being accepted as adults, both socially and in the eyes of the law. No adult should ever be sent to college by his parents or anyone else. Though his parents may provide financial assistance if they are able, he should go to college of his own volition, motivated by his own personal goals—or he should not go at all.

As a nation, we must decide how many of our young people, and which ones, should be afforded an opportunity for higher education and encouraged to pursue it. Because the decision will affect the welfare of the entire nation, and because the support for higher education must come from the people, the decision cannot be left to educators alone. It must concern us all.

III. THE STRUGGLE FOR REFORM

EDITOR'S INTRODUCTION

If the preceding sections of this compilation are any guide, the problems confronting today's colleges go far deeper than the momentary disruptions posed by "stagflation" or even the longer-term threat posed by shrinking enrollments. There are clear indications that students suspect that they are being swindled, that the value of their degrees is being rapidly deflated. "Credentialism"—the tendency of more and more employers to demand this or that degree or diploma for more and more kinds of jobs—is debasing the real value of all degrees and diplomas. Wily students can be forgiven for suspecting that college is little more than a trap designed to hold them off the overburdened job market for a few years.

There is a sense of malaise and discontent among faculty as well. Events of the sixties have eroded their authority, and they are not sure whether that is good or bad. Highly trained men and women find themselves teaching courses in remedial English and mathematics at sub-high-school levels. Some find it a challenge. Others are naturally perplexed. Is this what a Ph.D. has brought them to? And now, before the reforms of the sixties have been thoroughly evaluated, they are being goaded to ponder reforms even more fundamental in nature.

One could say that the challenges are not stirring a vigorous response, that faculty and students alike are divided and demoralized. The articles in this section tend to belie that conclusion, however. In its report on reforms of the 1960s, *U.S. News & World Report* indicates that students are at last being treated as adults, faculty members are finding a new commitment to teaching, and both are exhibiting a willingness to experiment without sacrificing academic standards. Though more pessimistic in tone, the second article, by Professor Charles Frankel of Columbia, shows that a fundamental restructuring of a "worn-out model" in higher education is now required and within the capacity of dedicated teachers. Martin Mayer in the third article, from *Commentary*, offers a far from negative view of the experience gained thus far by the City University of New York with its open admissions program. And in the last article, an editor of *Saturday Review/World* recounts both the benefits and setbacks involved in the radical curriculum reform adopted by Brown University in 1969, concluding that the experiment has been a success on the whole.

GHOSTS OF THE SIXTIES [1]

Reprinted from *U.S. News & World Report.*

Widespread reforms in US higher education, growing out of the campus uprisings of the 1960s, are now producing many surprises.

Some reforms—among them introduction of "pass-fail" in place of conventional grading—are clearly falling out of favor with students as well as faculty members.

Other changes, such as a stronger voice for students in academic policy making, are gaining wide acceptance.

On still other experiments, such as letting students design their own courses, the jury is still out.

Over all, these impressions emerge from a sampling of US campuses:

Anyone visiting a university for the first time since the early 1960s might get a few shocks. Coed dormitories are commonplace. Young couples, with little hindrance, often live together openly off campus. Students drop out for a term or a year, or change schools far more casually than was the case before rebellion hit the campuses.

Yet an adult visiting a university for the first time since

[1] From "Report Card on All those Campus Reforms of the '60s." *U.S. News & World Report.* 76:39-40. My. 6, '74.

the late 1960s also would find that today's postrevolutionary students show little mood for confrontation with authorities. Many are zeroing in on preparation for careers—and enrollment in professional schools is booming.

Dr. Dankwart A. Rustow, Distinguished Professor of Political Science at the City University of New York, cites these major shifts of recent years:

☐ College students now are being treated as adults for the first time.

☐ Many faculty members are finding "a new commitment to teaching."

☐ There is a willingness to experiment, but without sacrificing academic standards.

Black studies are still popular, along with women's studies and courses on ethnic origins. At the same time, there has been a winnowing out of hastily conceived courses of little interest to students—or prospective employers.

The results of the 1960s' rebellion against "lock step" education are evident everywhere.

Colleges, more and more, are permitting students to initiate new courses in which they demonstrate a special interest—one way, educators say, of keeping curricula up to date.

At Trinity College, in Hartford, Connecticut, J. Ronald Spencer, dean for community life, said students can work with faculty members on individually tailored courses. Between four hundred and five hundred such independent studies now are going on at Trinity.

Stanford University is offering studies in pollution, crime, prison reform, homosexuality and other current topics.

Hundreds of colleges have adopted the one-month winter term in which students can undertake independent and offbeat study—either on or off the campus, and often completely unrelated to their major academic fields.

Many colleges and universities, such as the University of

California and the University of Washington, are abandoning foreign-language study as a prerequisite for graduation.

Many if not most universities and colleges have reduced their lists of required studies for freshmen and sophomores—and some have abolished such requirements altogether.

Lawrence University, a liberal-arts institution in Appleton, Wisconsin, has eliminated most required courses for freshmen. It also permits a student to forgo all formal courses and requirements as long as the student sets up a four-year plan of individual study and research acceptable to the faculty.

However, Dean Thomas E. Headrick reported:

"Not very many students are interested in trying this kind of freedom."

Back to Basics

Also discerned on US campuses is a desire for a more structured education than has been offered at the more innovative universities in recent times.

The most experimental courses, sometimes called "finger painting" courses by cynical undergraduates, are reported to be not nearly as popular now as a few years ago. Some of these, critics said, were little more than "bull sessions" with no specific intellectual merit.

On the other hand, resurgent interest is developing in professional training.

Law and medical schools, in recent years, have been able to take only a fraction of applicants. Schools of dentistry and pharmacy are approaching the same status, and there are some signs that schools of business administration are once again rising in students' esteem after a period of disfavor with "relevance seeking" young people.

Today's students, too, are looking askance at reforms in grading which came as a result of complaints in the 1960s about "arbitrary" and "meaningless" judgments on students' work.

Many colleges still offer pass-fail grading as an option in

all courses, or at least in some electives. But, on a number of campuses, students are worrying about the adverse effect of this system on their chances of winning acceptance to a graduate school or job of their choice.

Said President William E. Kerstetter of DePauw University in Greencastle, Indiana:

"Many graduate schools look favorably on a record of good grades and unfavorably on pass-fail marks. As a result, many students disregard the pass-fail opportunities here."

Similar indications of returning support for the ABC system of grading turned up even at Antioch College, a highly innovative school in Yellow Springs, Ohio, where Dr. Francis T. Williams, Jr., associate professor of chemistry and an adviser to some premedical students, reported:

"It seems a lot of medical schools do not want to read our student evaluations, which have been written by our professors in lieu of grades. Consequently, a lot of our students are asking for grades in our science courses."

Student evaluation of teachers is still going on at some schools. At others, interest in the practice is waning—and it has all but faded out of the picture at Indiana University.

Yet at the University of Oregon, evaluation by students has become a fixture and is given weight in the promotion of faculty and the awarding of tenure. At the University of Washington, there is a formal office of student ratings.

Bigger Voice for Students

At one institution after another, however, this seems clear:

Recognition of today's students as grownups has led to giving them a much larger voice than ever before in running America's universities and colleges, and in establishing the pattern of their own education.

Most institutions now have student representatives on permanent committees. Some have students voting on the board of regents. At New York University, students hold about 25 percent of the seats in the university senate. NYU

President James M. Hester called the enhanced role of students in governance "most significant."

Given more authority and the responsibility that goes with it, students of the 1970s seem more willing to work within the system, campus administrators say. Dr. Charles G. Morris, an associate dean at the University of Michigan, commented: "I think the 1960s made our present students aware of how nonproductive, disruptive and dangerous mass protest is."

At Kent State University in Ohio, where four young people were shot to death during a student confrontation with the National Guard in 1970, more than two thousand students now are involved in volunteer work.

Young men and women seem to be taking their education seriously because it is more expensive and jobs are harder to find after graduation. Student-body president Steve Golvach at Rice University said:

"A great deal of the concern of the 1970s student is directed toward the welfare of that student after he gets out of college.

"He is not as tempted to jeopardize that as before. Too, students have found there is nothing really romantic about being a radical any more."

Hugh M. Satterlee, dean of students at the University of Illinois at Champaign-Urbana, adds a comment:

"The only facet of the 1960s that students here would like to return to would be the tuition costs."

Illinois has retained almost unchanged the academic reforms that grew out of the period of student unrest, according to Harold W. Hake, associate vice chancellor.

At the other extreme, academic reforms at Florida State University are seen by some students and professors as withering on the vine.

An advisory council and budget commission, set up to give students, faculty and staff a stronger voice, is inactive. A student court set up to determine punishment for viola-

tors of campus rules has had its jurisdiction narrowed and
now hears only minor cases.

Few in higher education believe that the changes now
seen on America's campuses have solved many of their long-
standing problems.

Some critics, such as Columbia University's Charles
Frankel, professor of philosophy, feel that higher education
has yet to recover from the body blows of the 1960s. [See
following article.—Ed.]

Most, however, seem to share the thinking of Rice's dean
of students, Dr. F. A. Wierum. Because of the changes that
have taken place in higher education, he said, "we've all
mellowed."

REFORMING THE REFORMS [2]

The significance of the chapter in the history of higher
education which began ten years ago at Berkeley is still a
matter of dispute, but of one thing there can be little question: it has left the higher educational community in a state
of passivity, its imagination focused not on the problems or
possibilities of the future, but on the unpleasantness of the
recent past. In the public memory, the shouting and the fires
have been put away as essentially evanescent phenomena,
temporary in their causes and effects. In the minds of most
university teachers and administrators, however, something
very like a civil war has taken place, and they are living
through its aftermath.

Is the analogy with civil war inflated? To be sure. The
tendency to grandiosity was a not inconsiderable element in
making the uproars of the past decade as loud as they were.
The campus revolution was not honest-to-god. It was a cha-
rade, a protected piece of theater, a game. But there are

[2] From "Reflection on a Worn-Out Model," by Charles Frankel, Old
Dominion Professor of Philosophy and Public Affairs at Columbia University.
Daedalus. 103:25-32. Fall '74. Reprinted by permission of *Daedalus,* Journal of
the American Academy of Arts and Sciences, Boston, Massachusetts. Fall 1974,
American Higher Education: Toward an Uncertain Future.

games people play from which they never recover. The game played in colleges and universities during the last ten years was a passionate game, a game into which people threw themselves entirely and in which they thought their basic principles and honor were involved, a game from which they emerged exhausted and exposed, having revealed themselves to others and, worst of all, to themselves. It is not surprising, after this experience, that the academic world is obsessed with its traumas, and not in a mood to come actively or even intellectually to grips with its problems.

The present "calm," indeed, is better than the violence that preceded it, but that is about all that can be said in its favor. To begin with, it is less than universal. Toronto, Berlin, and Oxford, to take some not inconspicuous institutions, are still places where violent disruptions take place. They occur, too, in the United States. The calm, where it exists, is in the main the calm of numbness. Small sit-ins or brief ones are commonplace occurrences. Militant students can still keep people they do not like from speaking on their campuses. University presidents are verbally abused in public in ways unimaginable before the Berkeley uprising. People simply do not see the point of making an issue of such matters. That this situation can be described as a return to "normal" suggests what the last decade has done to university standards.

But perhaps the more important story is being told in developments that do not catch the public eye, and hardly catch, it would seem, even the eye of the academic world. Consider the following phenomena: grade inflation; the progressive elimination of foreign-language requirements from the curricula; the steady dilution even of mild distribution requirements; the regularity with which curricular reforms turn out to involve simply less reading and writing; the living conditions in dormitories, from which universities have almost entirely withdrawn their supervisory authority although they continue to pay the bills; the double-talk about quotas that are not quotas and *apartheid* that is not *apartheid*.

One may approve or disapprove of one or another of these developments. Not one, however, has been the product of a serious discussion of fundamentals; not one has been the product of a faculty initiative. They are decisions of expediency, made not out of conviction but dispiritedness. They betoken an indisposition to exercise authority and to lead, an absence of confidence, of will, of thought, a depth of demoralization, which, more than any other single matter, endangers the health and autonomy of higher education. Not even the lack of money is so serious. The professoriate, the permanent citizenry of universities, faces its future with its sense of community in tatters and its principles in disarray.

There could hardly be a worse time for it to choose to rest on its scars. For the issues that lie ahead are likely to have as profound and shaking an effect on colleges and universities as those through which we have just lived.

Worn-Out Model

The issues that lie ahead, in their net thrust and direction, have to do, I believe, with the mounting inadequacy of the standard model of higher education that we have inherited. It is the model of the four-year college, sheltering people between the ages of seventeen and twenty-two, and joined to a university network designed to provide advanced training to a more limited number of people. The faculties of such institutions, both college and university, are composed, according to the model, of scholar-teachers, most of whom are engaged in significant research. These faculties exercise sole *de facto* authority over the issuance of certificates and degrees and over the selection of their professional colleagues.

This institution, in the British and American traditions, has always been thought to have, particularly at its undergraduate level, a moral and civic function even more important, in all probability, than its intellectual one. "Piety," "virtue" were the words that used to be used to describe what colleges should teach. Now that the clergy has lost its authority to fill these words with a content that everyone will accept, we use more elastic ones like "leadership," "social concern," "democratic" or "humanistic" values, or, most stretchable of all, "socialization." The moral and civil function, however, has remained fundamental, and it has been connected with two others—the effort, through the college, to guide the student to that field in which he can combine the best use of his talents and the greatest service to society, and the effort to introduce the student to the world of learning in such a way that he sees it not simply as the plaything of scholars but as a vocation in the service of God or Man. This conception of the moral and civic purpose of higher education, and its role in expanding individual opportunity, has lain behind the American effort to open the colleges to as many qualified people as possible, and to take the word "qualified" as standing for character and motivation, and not simply, or even mainly, for intellectual promise.

The classic model of higher education, however, has been a hybrid since the time, approximately a century ago, that the continental model of the graduate school, devoted to the intensive advancement of scholarship and the learned professions, was superimposed on the Anglo-Saxon model of the undergraduate college. Neither the graduate training of undergraduate teachers nor the prestige and promotion systems in which they work habituate them to see themselves as counselors or tutors in the virtues. The increasing specialization and sophistication of the fields of learning, and the more uncompromising demands for precise skills made by the economy, provide other strong reasons why higher education, at all levels, has been forced to attach more importance to sheer intellectual performance. Actual practice has been a compromise between these two functions (not to speak of others), and the model of a good higher education has also been a compromise, as suggested by phrases like "the well-rounded man" descriptive of its putative goal. Nor do I say this to complain. Any educational model not the work of zealots will recognize the diversity of human interests to be served, and will need to strike some balance among them.

Finally, because it has been perceived to have a transcendent moral as well as intellectual purpose, which external intrusions can damage, the model university has possessed a quasi-feudal status. Like a manorial estate, or a town with a charter of established privileges, it has had a hierarchial status-system, parental and governmental responsibilities toward its members, its own codes of conduct, and its own not inconsiderable sanctions to aid in their enforcement. Moreover, even when it has been entirely tax-supported, it has enjoyed, within broad limits, autonomy from the government and the courts.

This, of course, is a *model*. The majority of American institutions officially accredited as schools of postsecondary instruction were not more than faint approximations of it even before 1964. Nevertheless, what I have described has been, I think, the effective *norm*. The pressure was on institutions to try to live up to it, and if they differed from it, they were felt to be, and felt themselves to be, less than full-fledged members of the higher educational world. In the fifties and early sixties, for example, a long procession of two-year teachers' colleges was converted into four-year liberal arts colleges in deference to this conception of the normal and desirable.

Is this model adequate? To recover the power of self-direction, it seems to me, the higher educational community has to ask itself, deliberately and in the context of a sustained and controlled discussion and debate, what parts of this model can and should be preserved, what parts discarded, and what parts supplemented by quite different ideas of the normal and desirable.

Reshaping the Model

I shall have to be brief, almost telegraphic, in suggesting my own beginning thoughts about these questions.

The Late-Adolescent School. The notion that the predominant norm for higher education should be the college and university for students seventeen to twenty-five must almost certainly go by the board. A college education is no longer a rare commodity. For many middle- and upper-class students it has been converted from a prerogative into a duty, somewhere in between unintelligible, boring, and onerous. The signs grow that many are looking for alternatives to it. Moreover, our higher educational institutions, for a long time, have had more married students, older students, and more students working full time on the outside than the traditional model has supposed. Most of these people, however, have been in municipal institutions and community colleges that rate, in the traditional perspective, as not-quite-really colleges. In this way the ratings within our educational system have given implicit endorsement to prevailing forms of social and economic stratification.

The inherited norm seems to me bad both for the universities and for equality of opportunity. Why should the institutions with the greatest access to distinguished scholarship and advanced research facilities be so largely restricted to students in the years seventeen to twenty-five, a considerable number of whom have only the vaguest idea of why they are where they are? The rearrangement of scholarship programs, living arrangements, and curricula to provide, say, one third of the places in residential universities to people of twenty-five, thirty, or older, might represent a more efficient and economical use of expensive resources, a fairer distribution of educational opportunity, and a stabilizing and energizing change in the composition of student bodies.

The effects of the traditional model are visible, and their desirability challengeable. In seeking greater equality of opportunity, the policy of the colleges has been to seek to offer to hitherto disadvantaged seventeen-year-olds an opportunity to participate in that idyll of youth which, in imagination, the colleges have offered to middle- and upper-class young people. But the chance to choose people who have had jobs, and who have demonstrated, by their performance and the efforts they have made to continue their education, that they have the requisite equipment and motivation, offers a surer way of finding the right people, and strikes at a central reason for the maldistribution of educational achievement. The burden that poverty and deprivation put on the individual is that he takes longer, usually, to discover his opportunities and abilities. The chance to reenter the educational system at an older age is thus of particular value to the disadvantaged.

The Norm of Uninterrupted Schooling. Closely connected to the traditional notion of colleges and universities as the preserves of the young is the idea that an education, ideally, ought not to be interrupted. The departures from this ideal increase: the undergraduate leave of absence; the year between college and graduate or professional school; the periods of retraining required by industry; the return of married women to school and the job market when their children are grown.

But the change in the norm of uninterrupted schooling is called for, I suspect, by more than such trends. Colleges, a generation ago, were populated mainly by students in two categories—the children of the privileged, who knew they were making the friends and learning the manners appropriate to people of station, and the upwardly mobile, jealous for position and eager not to throw their opportunities away. For both groups the parental disciplines of the classic college were more than bearable. They knew why they were going to school, knew that they had to go through this mill to be considered as having arrived at adulthood, and found their status as people at a halfway station both intelligible and agreeable.

This inner reserve from which the authority of the college as a communal political entity was largely drawn is now depleted. The greater affluence and changed social standards of our present society have brought to the colleges a large number of students who do not regard themselves as the children of a privileged elite (although many of them are), but who are not on the way up either. They do not expect to improve on their father's position, and many would hope not to have to live as he has. For such students a college education of the old style can seem like a sustained period of hanging in the void. They see themselves as being in college only because of parental and social pressure. Only those with active intellectual interests are likely to know why they are where they are, and these often find themselves frustrated by the diversions, distractions, and flim-flam of an institution in which they are a minority. Combined with the possibility of easy reentry into universities at later ages, a policy of allowing young people to leave, of removing from them the pressure that the normal expectation is that they stay, should help create university populations with many fewer conscripts. We would do well to replace the norm of uninterrupted schooling, I think, by the norm of permanent and recurrent education, joined to the provision of jobs and training experiences for the age-group seventeen to twenty-five.

The Civic Function of Higher Education. One reason for the special status of the "normal" liberal arts college is that it was traditionally thought to be the major, and almost the only, purveyor of secular moral instruction beyond the high school. But this thought has long since been bypassed by events. For better or worse, the mass circulation magazines, particularly those aimed at the richer 50 percent of the population which has had an education beyond the secondary level, exercise a powerful influence in this realm. They are, in the French expression, *l'école parallèle.* Equally to the point, and perhaps more encouraging, are developments in public television and the public-program activities of agencies like the National Endowment for the Humanities and the National Endowment for the Arts, which can, if sustained and enlarged, serve major educational roles. The community college and adult education have also removed the monopoly of the liberal arts college.

Still to be fully exploited for the purposes of civic education are the graduate and professional schools, although the latter, I believe, are less to be faulted than the former. It is odd to announce, at the undergraduate level, the glories of the humanities and the liberation to be gained from the study of the pure sciences, and then, at the graduate level, to give next to no attention to the larger social, human, and even intellectual significance of the specialized subjects studied. The notion that "general education" is an undergraduate concern and that a graduate school is professional not liberal is one of the expressions of the inherited hybrid model of higher education—Anglo-Saxon at the base, continental at the top.

Preserving Diversity

"Elitist" and "Democratic" Higher Education. The distribution of the function of civic education more generously throughout the higher educational system makes possible another adjustment—the unapologetic concentration, by some colleges and universities, on the training of the 10 to 15 percent of the population equipped to make intellectual contributions to the arts, sciences, and learned professions. The present drift is relentlessly toward homogenization and the destruction of the most precious of all the characteristics of American higher education, its diversity. One reason for this drift is the dominance of the single model of the proper higher educational institution. It rapidly becomes an all-purpose model, making all distinctions fuzzy.

The question, of course, is whether the American public, with its egalitarian perspective, will be prepared to accept a postsecondary educational system in which clear distinctions exist between different kinds of institutions. The answer, in part, is that it has been doing so for a long time. Another part of the answer, I think, is that an educational system offering a broader range of alternatives, operating under an ampler notion of the normal and desirable, and less exclusively designed for the young, would be a more democratic system, more usable by those hitherto shut out.

In any case, the problem of numbers is probably lessening. The issue for the future is not to meet the steadily growing demand from one age group for an education basically conceived after one model. The figure of 50 percent, which represents the approximate present proportion of youth enrolled in institutions of postsecondary education, may well be the highwater mark. The problem for the future is to find the right 50 percent, and to provide the ways and means for sorting them out and directing them to the school best suited for them.

The Teachers. In this setting, the continued idolatry of the Ph.D. and the image of the teacher as also a productive research worker make for profound trouble. The members of teaching staffs of postsecondary institutions number, I believe, over 400,000. It is a transparent pretense that most of them are engaged in significant research, or should be. It is merely an invitation to them, indeed, to look down on themselves when they perform their central task as teachers. Even in the most noted institutions, the quality and importance of research are spotty. Is teaching less important, less intellectually demanding, less an art to be mastered or an achievement to be admired and rewarded?

Moreover, the coming of mass higher education, together with the confrontationist spirit of the decade since Berkeley, has altered the traditions of informal self-government within faculties. Although professors live within inherited traditions that are consensual and deferential, and that give a central place to the individual's quality of work, the pressures for unionization mount, as do the centralizing and standardizing tendencies turned loose by the courts and legislatures. If the autonomy and tone of the higher educational system as a whole are to be kept, there must probably be a group of institutions from which collective bargaining remains excluded.

Higher Educational Autonomy. The classic model of higher education bids fair to become increasingly inapplicable in one respect in which it is indispensable that it be preserved. This is the assignment of autonomy to institutions of advanced learning. Colleges and universities are being pulled steadily into the central legal system. Their decisions are being made for them by the courts, legislatures, and bureaucracies. This is only in part because they are all more dependent on public funds. It is also a consequence of the fact that, thanks in good part to the decade of Berkeley, the internal governance of universities has been conceded to be a proper field for close external supervision. The cries of oppression have been heard; that scourge of injustice, the Nixon Administration, has come to the rescue. Universities receive less money than they used to do from the federal government, but, in recompense, they receive more paternal guidance and protection from sin.

The issue is the universities' basic ordering of their long-term obligations. Whatever the higher educational system's capacity or incapacity substantially to correct major social injustices by its own direct efforts alone, it is surely part of its mission not to perpetuate injustices in its own domain. But the remedies adopted must be proportionate to the wrongs to be cured and consistent with the universities' other obligations. In relation to racial and sexual discrimination, to come to particulars, the question must be asked whether public outcry, changed attitudes, and the heightened sensitivity to the issues of people within the higher educational community will not in most circumstances be sufficient to set things right, without adding the tender ministrations of government bureaucracies.

Practices like the [United States Department of Health, Education, and Welfare] HEW guidelines, which require university officials to explain their practices to suspicious functionaries and to work under presumptions of guilt, are nevertheless justified, it is said on their behalf, by their purposes. After all, they seek to root out racial and sexual discrimination, not Communists. But should we be prepared, in the name even of the best causes, to establish the habit in government of reading universities' files, and giving its advice-with-sanctions in regard to the selection of students and faculty? The cost can be university autonomy, and that autonomy is the indispensable prerequisite for the authority of the university in free societies and the performance of its unique role.

The questions that have been shrugged off while blunderbuss methods of achieving social purposes have been used are extraordinary. Do we think it is a good idea to domesticate, in universities, the habit of obedient conformity to political and bureaucratic pressures? What will universities be like after a generation of this sort of thing? And what assurance do we have that a future government will not use this power of inspection and punishment which has been conceded to it to promote causes for which the members of universities will have less sympathy? The Free Speech revolt, the war protests, the Movement, were not animated by trust of governmental authority. What they have accomplished is the strengthening of the power of the most conservative government in fifty years to send its inspectors into universities.

It is an accomplishment which goes hand in hand with the growth, within higher educational institutions, of the bloc system of governance and the adversary system of administration and justice. The vetoes have been multiplied, the power to decide and act reduced. No doubt the older model of a university, framed to stand *in loco parentis* for adolescent students, needs considerable modification; but the model of a university in which teachers and students are organized into blocs and treated as though they were competing social classes is not an improvement. It is laughable in itself, and it runs at cross purposes to the effort to make teaching and learning a cooperative process.

The restoration of more informal and consensual procedures of academic consultation and governance is indispensable, I believe, to the reactivation of effective university self-government. In the larger political community
it makes sense to provide elaborate procedures to ensure
that individuals are able to protect themselves against exploitation, deception, and oppression by others, and particularly the powerful. But the presumption that teaching
and studying ought to be carried on with the fear of *Homo
lupus* always present has never characterized civilized educational practices. In few institutions today, let us hope,
is it in fact the everyday working assumption. It is merely
the ritualistic one, written into the formal rules and procedures—which does not prevent it from blocking the processes of self-government.

History's Timetable

These reflections bring us back to the circumambient
issues with which we began—the higher educational community's present state of mind and morale, and, more
broadly, the recipient culture within which the discussion
and conduct of higher education goes on. In the years since
Berkeley we have had the chance to see some of that culture's special and disturbing faults. To the extent that they
persist, the outlook is dim for a reasoned solution to many
of the problems with which the colleges and universities are
confronted.

When I think back to the campus troubles, what rises to
the center of my mind is the sense they gave one of being
caught inside something with a momentum of its own. One's
colleagues, one's students seemed all to be reading from
scripts prepared in advance. One's university went to its
fate as though hypnotized, sleep-walking over the precipice.
Even now, at some years' remove, the impression that events
followed a set path is fortified, not weakened. The degree
to which the stories that unfolded on different campuses

were similar is remarkable. A Platonic Idea of a campus revolution migrated from institution to institution, at each place issuing its commands and finding its obedient soldiers. Even differences in national educational traditions only slightly affected the relentless unoriginality of behavior. The slogans, alternatives, factionalisms, and compromises rehearsed at Berkeley and Columbia were rehearsed as well at Florence, Copenhagen, and Amsterdam.

What was it that gave events this headless momentum and common direction? I think it was the environing culture of higher education, the eyes that interpreted what was happening, the ears that heard the words, the mouths that formed the responses. The common culture took what was happening, read its own prepared meaning into it, and gave the play back to the actors to take their cues. "All of us," wrote Raymond Aron, about his experiences in Paris in 1968, "played a role in that period. I begin with myself, I freely say so, I played Tocqueville, which is not without a touch of the ridiculous, but others played Saint-Just, Robespierre or Lenin, which, all things considered, was even more ridiculous." Perhaps people in Paris were somewhat more aware of whom they were impersonating than were people in America, but, if so, that is the principal difference.

The press is part, but only part, of the process by which events are kneaded into their stereotypes. The journalists come to a campus in trouble, listen to both sides, which is their job, give a hearing and, with it, significance and legitimacy to groups that have been obscure before, and thus change the balance of power and authority. More, they particularize the stories, telling their who, what, when, and where, all in the singular, and encouraging the misapprehension that what is taking place is an event local in its causes and manageable if local reforms are made. Worst of all, however, they are in a hurry, they must make their deadlines, they are only human, and there is nothing like an ideology à la mode to help in putting a story together and giving it a meaning. So the press and the media line up the disputants in the university: the conservatives vs. the progressives, the old vs. the young, the powerful vs. the helpless, the selfish vs. the idealistic. What can each man do but play his part?

Moreover, the ideology fades into the ideology that has spread into most of the empty spaces in the contemporary academic mind. Words have ritualistic uses. *Change, innovation, experimentation* are treated as automatically eulogistic terms. In this context all ambiguities in political nomenclature disappear as well. *Liberal* means, quite simply, the espousal of the new and therefore the better. *Radical* means the same thing, but with more impatience or perhaps more sincerity. *Conservative,* by contrast, means hankering after the old and the worse—an attitude, needless to say, which is inexplicable in an intelligent man unless he is selfish and protecting his privileges. Once this vocabulary is sprinkled like powder over all issues, some stirring gymnastics are possible. One remains a "liberal" though one would deny the right to free speech to those with whom one disagrees; or one is labeled "conservative" because one does not think curricula should be redesigned to introduce the insights of the encounter movement. No issue is examined on the merits. Each is pegged into the timetable of history.

And history, of course, is like a well-trained regiment that moves in a straight line across a field. This presumption, too, colors the meaning of ideas and events. Thus, if one opposes racial discrimination, one ought also to oppose discrimination of rights and functions between young and old, or students and teachers. If one is of the opinion that redistribution of income is the wave of the future, one ought also to favor fewer classroom hours and more field trips, for that is the wave of the future, too. The basic paradox, said a writer in *Le Monde,* describing an international meeting of scholars to discuss the university emergency, is that so many of these people are "liberals" in politics and "conservatives" in education. Whether the conservatism amounted to more than a desire to preserve liberal principles of free speech and independent inquiry the author did not say. History will not put up with two-facedness.

The protection and reform of higher education will thus require something more than only specific programs. It will require a professoriate more concentrated on its common tasks and obligations, more ironically self-aware of what it has contributed to its own troubles, and better able to protect itself against its own vulgarisms.

OPEN ADMISSIONS FOR ALL? [3]

In New York City, up until the late 1960s selection to the free, tax-supported City University (which enrolled about 140,000 students in 1969) was made according to high school grades, supposedly uniform across all the city's schools. In 1920, a graduate with a 72 average would have gained entry to City College, recently promoted to postsecondary status; by the late 1960s, most of the four-year colleges in the city system were requiring an 82 average, which in effect meant the top 40 percent of the city's high school graduates (or the top sixth of the age group, academically, because three fifths of the city's adolescents do not complete an academic program in an academic high school). For entrance to the city's two-year junior colleges (locally called community colleges, though none in fact drew from a geographically restricted area), requirements were generally much lower: a 70 average, which was earned by almost 90 percent of all graduates from the high schools.

Thus, though neither a "general" high school diploma nor a vocational diploma granted automatic entrance to any college, City University was deep in the social-mobility business long before the day of Open Admissions; at all

[3] From "Higher Education for All? The Case of Open Admissions," by Martin Mayer, author of *The Schools;* an authority on trends in higher education. *Commentary.* 55:37-47. F. '73. Reprinted by permission of Curtis Brown, Ltd. Copyright © 1973 by the American Jewish Committee.

times in its history, 90-odd percent of its entering freshmen
were from homes where neither parent had attended college.
The fact is, however, that these entering freshmen were not
themselves "representative" of the high school population as
a whole. The "general" program in the high schools was
heavily black (and Puerto Rican), and in both high school
grades and in competitive exams, black students consistently
ranked lower than white students. With increasing frequency
since the 1940s, educators and social reformers have been
drawing baleful correlations between the preponderance of
whites in the universities and in the seats of the mighty. At
one level, promoters of the black cause began to demand
greater opportunities for blacks to move up the educational
ladder; at another level, spokesmen began to insist that educational barriers, especially competitive examinations of any
kind, be removed from the forward march of the black
young.

At first these pressures concentrated on improvement of
secondary education: New York's much advertised Higher
Horizons project of the 1950s was started by a junior-high-
school principal who had discovered that only about 4 percent of the graduates of his school went on to college. Programs like Higher Horizons produced a steady but fairly
slow expansion in the number of blacks proceeding to college. In 1964, the Economic Opportunity Act made the recruitment of blacks a prime goal of the poverty program,
and New York funded its first College Discovery venture.
The federal government dropped the other shoe in 1965 in
promulgating the Higher Education Act, and a year later
the state funded the Search for Education, Elevation, and
Knowledge (SEEK) program, by which students from poor
neighborhoods who were not otherwise eligible for regular
admission to the City University four-year colleges were accepted into, and paid to attend, special programs run more
or less by the colleges and designed to remedy deficiencies
in skills and attitudes.

In 1969, nevertheless, a New York City school system

that was more than half black and Puerto Rican in student composition was still feeding into a four-year college system that was less than one-tenth black and Puerto Rican. Economic conditions in the city, coupled with the immense demographic bulge of the age-classes born shortly after World War II, meant that a majority of "minority" college-age New Yorkers not in college were unemployed. Especially where the colleges were located in slums, pressure to do something for the young people of the neighborhood had become very strong.

At this time the Board of Higher Education, the controlling body of City University (appointed by the mayor), began a number of studies looking toward the day when the university would undertake to accept *all* graduates of the city's high schools, regardless of their performance in high school or their achievement in examinations. In general, the evidence turned up by these studies was discouraging: the centerpiece, an examination of the high school senior class by Vice-Chancellor Robert Birnbaum, produced a well-documented opinion that virtually every New York City high school graduate reasonably ready for an ordinary college program was already going to college. Nevertheless, both Mayor Lindsay and City University Chancellor Albert Bowker felt a political need to affirm the eventual establishment of an Open Admissions program, to take effect some time in the mid-1970s—a date far enough in the future to ensure that their successors rather than they themselves would be stuck with the problem.

The model originally in mind was the California state system, with its three tiers of higher education: the universities, which accept the top 12 percent of each high school graduating class; separate four-year colleges, which take the balance of the top half; and the two-year junior colleges, which take the rest (plus some nongraduates of high schools). Among the drawbacks of this arrangement is the heavy concentration of blacks and Chicanos in California's junior colleges (a concentration that tends to get heavier as progress is made in desegregating the high schools: the top half of an all-black school is, of course, all black, while the top half of the high school graduating class nationwide, as measured by standardized tests, is only about 3 percent black). Such imbalances have consequences: the Black Panther party started at predominantly black Merritt Junior College a few miles down the road from what was an almost entirely white University of California at Berkeley. In New York, the planners had to consider also the fate of the students at the city's four selective-entrance college preparatory high schools. Most of the students who ranked in the bottom 10 percent of the graduating class at the Bronx High School of Science, for example, were better prepared for college than most of the students in the top 10 percent of some of the other high schools.

Moreover, if one assumed—as one had to assume—that the great majority of newcomers taken into the four-year colleges under any new program could not routinely handle college work, it was necessary to devise means of helping them catch up. Sensibly, Bowker took an interest in secondary education, and tried to arrange to have five public high schools put under the wing of City University, to experiment with new programs. Some work was already being done, through a program called College Discovery Prong II, in which university professors and students were working with about 1,500 high school students selected in the ninth grade for their *unlikelihood* of proceeding to college. The citywide Council Against Poverty had sabotaged this project in a fit of pique against the school system, withdrawing the $5 weekly grant the students had been paid in the first years of the experiment, and the Board of Education was being unhelpful, but the students were coming along much better than would have been anticipated from their ninth-grade academic and psychological test scores. Given actual control of some schools, the unversity might, just possibly, have been able to bring greater numbers of "disadvantaged" students up to the minimum levels of skill required for college.

Direct Action by Militants

But the Board of Education was unwilling to turn over control of any school (it still is), and in 1969 circumstance outran planning. In May, a small group of black students, abetted and probably led by militants from the neighborhood, "seized" the South Campus of City College on the western edge of Harlem. They chained the gates closed and themselves to the gates, vowing to remain in adverse possession until the Board of Higher Education met the five "demands" of the "movement." The most important of these demands entailed a vast increase in the still small number of black and Spanish-speaking students at a college located in an exclusively black and Puerto Rican section of the city.

Confronted with a court order, the demonstrators disappeared, but the situation they had dramatized did not. "It was not only the blacks," says Frederick L. Burkhardt, president of the American Council of Learned Societies, who was then president of the Board of Higher Education. "It was the eight-thousand-dollar-a-year whites, saying, 'We pay our taxes. We want to go to college, and we have the right to go to college.' It was a demand that was irresistible." City University Vice-Chancellor Seymour Hyman, an alumnus of City College's student body and professorate, remembers a slightly different scenario: "I got a call from Al Bowker—he was at a meeting somewhere and couldn't leave it, and there had been a report over the radio that the Great Hall of City College had been set on fire. I went up there, and I saw the smoke pouring from the windows. We had a meeting that night, and I was telling people about what I felt when I saw that smoke coming out of that building, and the only question in my mind was, How can we save City College? And the only answer was, Hell, let everybody in. . . ."

The compromise was worked out by Robert Birnbaum, a tall, elegant young man whose manner is closer to that of the Ivy League than to that of the City University. Allen Ballard, then head of the SEEK program at City—black, a former student of Merle Fainsod's at Harvard—was fighting for a compensatory approach and a quota for "third-world" students (at least half of all entrants to City College). Others, politically more aware, were urging an expansion of SEEK, a sheltered college-within-a-college, rather than a quota system that would exclude "qualified" whites for the benefit of "unqualified" blacks. Birnbaum suggested that every high school graduate be admitted to some branch of City University, even if his high school work had been in a nonacademic program, but also that everyone who would previously have qualified for one of the four-year colleges be guaranteed his place, and that the freshman classes at these colleges be expanded drastically to secure a better ethnic mix.

The formula Birnbaum worked out, which has been operative starting with the high school graduating class of June 1970, was complicated and in the end not as effective as he and the board had hoped. Each graduating senior from the city's high schools lists in rank order the colleges he would like to attend. For each college, the computer takes the first choices, up to the numbers accepted in 1969 (or half the total for the next year, if that figure is larger), simply by running down the grade levels. This produces a cutoff grade by college, and by program within the college if the programs admit separately (as engineering and nursing do, for example). In 1972, the cutoff grade for entry to Queens College (the highest) was 85; the cutoff grade for entry to City College was 77.5. The rest of the class is filled with students who did not achieve the cutoff grade but did achieve a rank in the graduating class of their own high school matching the citywide percentage of students who *did* achieve the cutoff grade. Thus, 23 percent of the city's graduating seniors in 1972 averaged 85 or better, so anyone in the top 23 percent of his own high school class, regardless of his grades, was acceptable at Queens College. Sixty percent of the city's graduating seniors averaged 77.5 or better, so anyone in the top 60 percent of his graduating class was taken at City College—if City was his first choice or if he had failed to get in at his first choice and City was his second choice.

In general, the community colleges take what is left, though some students who could go to four-year colleges choose to attend a community college nearer their homes (transfer from community college to senior college is now automatic if a community-college graduate wishes to continue, so a student may feel he has nothing to lose by starting off in the neighborhood); and a few of the programs at the community colleges (nursing at New York City Community College in Brooklyn, for example) are so popular that their entrance requirements are higher than those of City College.

Birnbaum's scheme required that the entering classes at all the four-year colleges be substantially expanded—doubled, potentially. And if the high school grades meant what they seemed to mean, new courses and programs would have to be developed to give the newcomers any chance at all. What the City College protesters had demanded, after all, was not access to higher education but possession of diplomas; they were not willing to accept what they called the "revolving door" approach of the Midwest land-grant colleges, where a third to a half of each entering class is flunked out before the end of the freshman year.

The man charged with finding or inventing and determining the cost of these programs was David Newton, dean of Baruch College, a former City College psychology professor and a tough-minded believer in his job. He is now vice-chancellor in charge of personnel for City University, and has been handling management's end of the interminable contract negotiations with the faculty union. ("As a reward for distinguished service in setting up the Open Admissions program and starting York College in Queens," he says, "I have been sent to Vietnam.") In retrospect, Newton is less than proud of the performance of his committee: "We were given less than a year, and one of the initial cues was that we weren't properly funded. And the sense of commitment and dedication I had expected from my colleagues was nowhere to be found." But in any event, there was not much Newton and his committee could order people to do: they had no power. Each of the eighteen colleges in City University is essentially autonomous, appointing its own faculty, offering its own courses, allocating the money it receives from headquarters according to its own perception of budgetary needs (except that everyone must live by the city-wide union contract). Each was to make its own decisions as to the severity of the problems represented by Open Admissions, and devise its own programs accordingly. All Newton's committee could do was recommend an allocation of an extra $400 per student for special services (over and above the $1,700 per student that was in 1969–70 the standard budget formula), and suggest a reading of the literature of remediation (none of which is much good). "The only thing I regret," Newton says, "is our failure to spend money to research and develop new educational techniques and curricula."

You had a faculty asked all of a sudden to do something they didn't know anything about [says Chancellor Robert Kibbee, who arrived from Pittsburgh in 1971 to find Open Admissions in existence]. Even those who thought they knew couldn't conceive how badly many of these kids were prepared. Nobody knew really what he was doing. The combination of compassion and disbelief—and people who thought it was a lousy idea—meant that the first year, and [grudgingly] the second year, were a hell of a mess. It takes a lot of time to recover from a start like that.

Some Initial Results of Open Admissions

In 1969, City University admitted a freshman class of just under 19,000; in 1970, the total was just under 35,000. At the time, a City University press release trumpeted the "fact" that the 1969 proportions had shown only 14 percent black and Puerto Ricans, while the 1970 entrants were 33 percent black and Puerto Rican; subsequent investigation showed that the 1969 proportion had actually been 19.7 percent, and the 1970 proportion was only 26.2 percent. Of the increase of 16,000 in the number of freshmen, "others" made up 10,000; and today's visitor to remedial courses at Hunter and Baruch will find them overwhelmingly white (less so at City and [in 1973] at Brooklyn). All high school seniors applying to City University in 1970 were asked to take standardized tests for diagnostic purposes. The results showed that there were a few hundred Open Admissions students who did not in fact need remedial work in English or math—and no fewer than 6,000 regularly admitted students who *did.* (An effort was made to keep the scores on this test secret, but the figures leaked to the *Times,* and since then, to avoid similar publicity, each college has been told to administer its own test, the results of which are not collated at headquarters.) It is a sobering thought that in 1970 one quarter of the entrants to City University who had earned grades of 80 or better in the city's high schools scored below the national average for twelfth-graders on a standardized reading test.

At some colleges, efforts were made to handle the influx of unprepared students by tutoring alone. Weaker freshmen were counseled to take fewer than the usual number of courses, and urged to try music-appreciation or sociology rather than chemistry or modern language; in addition, "buddies" were assigned from the ranks of upper-classmen to offer help on an unstructured basis. At most colleges, some special remedial coures in English and math were organized. Typically, these courses did not in the first year carry college credit; but today they do, almost everywhere in the City University system (job-oriented New York City Community College and Baruch College, once the business-school division of City College, are notable exceptions).

The decision to give college credit for what is often junior-high-school work has most often been taken strictly as a result of pressure from desperately unhappy (one remedial teacher at Baruch says "demoralized") students who feel they are being asked to suffer and sweat "for nothing." But there have also been practical reasons. Hostos Community College in the Bronx, for example, has a twelve-hour-a-week "Libra" program (remedial English, black or Puerto Rican history, performing arts, and social science) for students whose reading scores fall below tenth-grade level on entrance to college. Its "unique feature," says Zane Rodriguez, the young chairman of the Hostos English Department, "is the credit-bearing remediation concept. The students can earn nine credits the first semester for the twelve hours. The Veterans Administration, Model Cities, and the union all require that students take twelve hours and earn nine credits to be eligible for benefits. Libra keeps them eligible."

At City College, the argument has been that the college's requirement of 128 credits for graduation is the highest in the city, and the awarding of credits for remedial courses is merely a way to bring City into line with its sister schools. At LaGuardia Community College, President Joseph Shenker takes the position that "the remedial program is part of the regular curriculum and we give credit for everything." Hunter gives only one (rather than three) credits for the lowest-level reading course; only two for the upper-level reading course. But Queens, like LaGuardia, has decided that a course is a course, and its 40 freshmen who entered in 1972 with high-school grade averages below 76 (out of an entering class of 2,600) will receive a full semester's credit for a program of Reading 1; Remedial English 01; Contemporary Civilization, on a low reading level; and a fourth course of their own choosing (something in the art or music field is recommended).

Innovations in Community Colleges

Two of the new community colleges—Hostos, opened in 1970, and LaGuardia, opened in 1971—are operated on original principles designed in large part to help Open Admissions students, defined for community-college purposes as students whose grade average in high school is under 75 or whose preparation is in nonacademic secondary programs. Such students constitute the majority of entrants at both of these colleges.

LaGuardia, located in a converted Sperry Rand factory in Long Island City, describes itself as the first co-op community college. Its academic year is divided into four quarters, and students must commit themselves for all four (teachers work three quarters). An entering freshman takes two quarters as a full-time student, and in his third quarter the college finds him a nine-to-five job, most frequently in a retail store, a city office, a bank, or an insurance company. The public schools also hire some students, and this fall ten LaGuardia students were in Puerto Rico working as teacher aides. The employer's reports on his work at the job become part of the student's academic record; LaGuardia keeps up with his progress through visits to the job site by a liaison staff and a "practicum," a two-hour evening seminar that meets six times during the student's quarter on the job. Attendance at the practicum is compulsory.

In his fourth quarter, the student returns to school full time; and in his second year he alternates quarters at school with quarters on the job (with a new practicum each time). Another LaGuardia innovation is an intensive week at the beginning of each academic quarter during which the student devotes full time to the study of a single urban topic, combining instruction and field observation in an *ad hoc* mix.

The current academic year is LaGuardia's second. Out of 550 students who started just after Labor Day in 1971, 400 were still matriculated when the current year began, but attrition in the students' fifth quarter (their second on a job) seems to have been higher than the college wants to admit. Students get unhappy at the department stores, where they are often used as stock boys and girls, and at the banks, where they typically start as teller trainees. Yet the job program, in the opinion of Harry Heinemann, the dean of the cooperative education division at LaGuardia, has educational advantages for both the students and the college quite apart from the money the students earn. "For our students, an educational experience means sitting on a chair and the teacher gives assignments—that's learning. Then there's the real world, which is different. We're giving them the idea that you learn from experiences on a job. Meanwhile, we can adjust our programs to the jobs available. . . ."

It would take much more time than I could spend at LaGuardia to form even a vague opinion about the chances for success of so new a program; the one practicum I attended was an infuriating disaster. About 70 percent of the staff at LaGuardia are experienced college teachers; the rest come from high schools. Remediation involves course work plus "study labs" with standard remedial materials. On one level at least, the cooperative program has been a measurable success—jobs were in fact found for everybody the first two times around. This spring, however, LaGuardia will need no fewer than 650 thirteen-week jobs for its students, and may not be able to find them. Shenker crosses his bridges one at a time.

Hostos represents an intellectually more radical venture than LaGuardia in adapting higher education to special needs. City University headquarters speaks of it as a college using programmed instruction and computer-assisted instruction as major elements, but in fact students are using neither programs nor computers. President Candido de Leon, a man in his late forties but much younger in appearance, developed the basic Hostos approach while working at the Board of Higher Education. (De Leon did not start the college himself; he was called back from sabbatical to rescue it after a disastrous first year.) The approach seeks to determine performance objectives for groups of brief "modules" which taken together constitute a course. Each module ends in a "milestone," an examination the student takes when he or she feels ready for it, at a separate testing center. Some of the descriptions of these courses, as they appear in the catalogue, are pretty sorry stuff: Sociology 1231, for example, carrying three credits—"The student will be able to define *or recognize* [emphasis added] terms related to social mobility, role, status, race prejudice, and factors leading to social change." And the tests given are nearly all teacher-tests administered when the teacher thinks the class should be ready—in standard academic style.

Hostos is located in a wretchedly crowded former factory loft in the Bronx; nearly 90 percent of its students are Open Admissions students by the under-75 grade-level definition. They are older on the average than students at most of the colleges. Many are primarily Spanish-speaking, and 70 of the college's 150 courses are offered in Spanish as well as in English. "The first-year students," de Leon says wearily, "were given the impression they could complete the entire program in Spanish. That was not my idea—they must have an intensive English program in case they wish to transfer; to tell them anything else would be irresponsible." The career emphasis at Hostos is on health services; de Leon is still appalled by his predecessor's notion that people could work effectively in responsible jobs in New York City hospitals without a good reading knowledge of English.

Probably because of de Leon, there are people of unusual distinction on the Hostos faculty. Among the mathematics professors is Mariano Garcia, a smiling white-haired man who was chairman of the mathematics department at the University of Puerto Rico, has written a Spanish-English math dictionary, and teaches in both languages. Lois Lamdrin, who supervises the English end of Hostos's Libra program, taught at Pittsburgh's Carnegie-Mellon before she came to New York. "When I started," she says, "I had all the white liberal biases about what these students could achieve if given complete freedom. We all lost those." Quite apart from questions of performance objectives, which still bedevil all those in the nonscience and nonvocational areas

at Hostos, work in English is now pretty thoroughly structured, with assignments like writing descriptions of photo-
graphs supplied by the instructor, and vocabulary lessons
like one relating to the five senses.

Most of what happens at Hostos is clearly not college
work, but some of it is. Students in a recorder class (learning musical staff notation for college credit!) are carrying
books which include *Four Ibsen Plays,* Bone's *Freshman
Calculus,* and Broom & Selznick's *Principles of Sociology.*
Almost inevitably, the college can show one really spectacular success: a Puerto Rican girl who got through the two-
year program in one year, then went on to Queens College
and got through her last two years of college in one year,
and now is back at Hostos teaching while doing graduate
work. Equally inevitably, the records are littered with failure; and the great majority of those who graduate are simply
not ready for the third year of a senior college, to which
they gain automatic entrance on presentation of the Hostos degree. Still, I for one will remember the hush that fell
on Mariano Garcia's math class as he came to something
his class found difficult but Professor Garcia said they had
to know.

Teaching Remedial English

At Baruch, some of the remedial work in English is tied
directly to course work in other subjects. (Similar procedures are apparently employed at Bronx Community College.) The remedial teachers, mostly former high school
(and junior high) teachers, are separate from the rest of the
faculty; most of the professors have taken the position that
the Open Admissions students will have to get through the
same courses everybody else gets through. ("Their expectations of what college freshmen should be able to do are
way high," says one of the remedial teachers, forgetting that
these expectations derive from experience with regularly
admitted students; one of the strengths, and dangers, of
good remedial teachers is that they become strong partisans

of their students.) So the remedial staff, now isolated in a freshmen-only annex where a high school used to be, schemes and works to get the Open Admissions students through the courses.

The device used is a "study lab," which gathers together as many as possible of the students with reading problems who are taking a given course. The teacher goes over the textbook for this course with groups of perhaps a dozen students, outlining the ideas and reinforcing the vocabulary, sometimes helping with papers and with the spotting of items likely to be on future exams. Many Baruch professors are less than enthusiastic about this procedure— "They're afraid you're touching their subject matter," says Stephen Urkowitz, an earnest young man who started in the Baruch remedial staff part time while working toward his Ph.D. in English literature, and has chosen to identify with the remedial teachers rather than with the English Department. Still, the fact is that Baruch Open Admissions students in some numbers are getting through the same courses that the best of the regularly admitted students are taking, and this is not happening at many colleges in City University.

Dean Ballard, who should know, says that "the best programs in English are kind of uniform." Last spring, more than six hundred teachers working in English remediation at City University met at the Hotel Commodore for a two-day weekend conference which presumably should have spread the word about any original or especially successful program. Hunter has gone in for a "sector analysis" approach, derived from linguistics, for the teaching of writing skills; Brooklyn College is reputed to have a "bidialectal" program for black students whose spoken English diverges drastically from standard English. But so far there have been no breakthroughs, no techniques that can be transferred down to the high schools, and the New York City high schools continue to deteriorate.

The failures of both student and program are often dis-

tressing to watch. Nearly three months into the academic
year, a group at Hunter was offered a lecture in how to use
the library, essentially an introduction to the arcana of the
Dewey Decimal System, which is part of the fifth-grade curriculum. The librarian asked how many of the class of
fifteen had used the library yet, and was rewarded by one
rather tentatively raised hand, by a girl who said that she
hadn't actually *used* it, but she worked at the library part
time. With the arrival of the first Open Admissions transfers
from community colleges to the four-year colleges, professors in upper-level courses are meeting utterly intractable
problems of sheer bewilderment in their students. "They've
been getting *A*'s," said one, "and they're devastated when
I have to give them *D*'s. Now what I do is show them an
A paper, and they're honest about it: they say, 'I just can't
do *that*.' But I'm not sure what good it does them." At
City College, where the administration has forbidden the
imposition of prerequisites, a larger than usual proportion
of the faculty has been making contact with truly hopeless
students, and have not the vaguest notion what they are
supposed to do about it.

Heavy Casualty Rates

Vice-Chancellor Hyman speaks approvingly of "compensatory courses," intermediate between remedial and regular:
"English 1, say, meets six times instead of three times a
week, and for twice the time and effort the student gets the
usual three credits." Tom Carroll, assistant dean of the
faculty at the New York City Community College, warns
against this approach on the basis of advice from California,
where he visited junior-college faculty who had been living with Open Admissions for a long time. "They all told
me," he says, "that if you attach a remedial course to a
regular course the whole course becomes remedial." What
can be said for certain is that the most publicized (and interesting) such venture, Chemistry 5-6-7 at City College, can
claim only very mixed results.

Chem 5 is the brainchild of Abraham Mazur, who has been at City for more than forty years, as a student and then as a professor, and who was chairman of the Chemistry Department when Open Admissions came about. Mazur's thesis was that Open Admissions students would be able to master the normal two-term first-year chemistry course if given three terms to do so, and that they would want to take such a course even though they could get only two-thirds credit for each semester's work. "Even the kid who was the worst prepared in high school," Mazur says, "who did badly and knew it, has the same ambition as the Jewish middle-class kid: he wants to be a doctor." The second part of the argument has proved entirely correct: enrollment in the first semester of Chem 5 has been high every term. But the first part is wrong: the students are in much worse shape, especially in mathematics, than Mazur had imagined. "I have identified kids," he says sadly, "who don't know that 373 over 273 is greater than one."

Of the 73 students who enrolled in the first semester in Chem 5, only 4 survived to enter the third semester—which is where college-level work begins. "By the spring of 1971," Mazur recalls, "it was clear we were facing a disaster." At a time when City College was removing *all* prerequisites to courses in the humanities and social sciences, Mazur arranged with the math department for an elementary algebra and remedial-arithmetic course that would henceforward be a prerequisite for students in Chem 5. By 1972–73, City College was giving full credit for each of the three semesters of Mazur's course (i.e., instead of working three semesters for two semesters' credit, the unprepared student now gets nine cedits for—ideally—the same work that earns the prepared student only six credits). Mazur also convinced the nursing department that the first two semesters of his course should be enough to meet nurses' requirements in chemistry, and enrollment in Chem 5 mounted to 190 in fall 1972. But in the third semester of the course there were still only 17 students, from an entry of 120 two terms before. And the first semester, which is all that most students enrolling in the course actually complete, is described by Mazur as "junior-high-school general science." It is in fact a little better than that—Boyle's Law, which I watched being taught to a rather unreceptive class, is not in most junior-high programs—but it isn't much better.

Ivo Duchacek's course on Political Ideas and Issues, offered only to Open Admissions students at City, is probably more demanding. Duchacek is a white-haired Czech refugee whose scholarly concern has been with the fate of his motherland, and he is not teaching for the purpose of radicalizing his students. (He is also not teaching the course for gain: he has donated it to City College, over and above his normal load.) Two English instructors work with him on the problems of twenty-seven students: they attend his classes and he attends theirs. All students are asked to read brief excerpts from material of some significance (mostly modern). The assignments are imaginative: in one, for example, Duchacek presents paragraphs by Fanon, Mao, Chiang, and Touré, and asks his students to write two sentences—"just two"—answering the question, "What anxiety is common to all these men?" Of the current group of 27 students, Duchacek feels he may have some chance with 22: "I'm really pleased with them—the only thing is, their English is awful." There were 70-odd in a similar class that year, and Duchacek reports that when he took over Professor Hans J. Morgenthau's work for a month this fall he found five former Open Admissions remedial students in Morgenthau's European theory course. "I watched them carefully and listened to their questions, and no doubt about it, they are 'in.'"

Elsewhere, courses with names like Political or Urban Ideas and Issues are likely to be taught by instructors who feel humble before their illiterate Third World students, to whom they believe will fall the honor of making the Revolution. Some of these courses lie below junior-high level: Hunter's first course in urban studies, for instance, sends students out on field trips to make color slides they will later screen for the class (rock music playing on a cassette as they go, to make the presentation multimedia). This is fourth-grade show-and-tell. "The course culminates," said one of its young teachers, "in change strategies—the whole idea of change." Even this stuff has its defenders. "Rhetoric," says Hans Spiegel, who set up the course, "is the first important rung up the abstraction ladder." But college is late in the game for a first step toward abstraction.

As for black-studies courses, many of these are doubtless "revolutionary" in tone; neither time nor patience permitted an investigation, and anyway, access is usually by invitation only. At both City and Hunter, and perhaps elsewhere, there is pressure to permit black and Spanish-speaking students to take all or nearly all their courses in a black-studies or Puerto-Rican studies department. This is not the place to hash over once again the pros and cons of such departments: clearly, there is a need for a black perspective in all social and historical studies; equally clearly, black-studies departments often become shelters for untalented students, and in education as in the economy, protective tariffs typically lead to overpriced and shoddy goods.

Winners and Losers

In an article in *City Almanac* last summer [1972], Joe L. Rempson of Bronx Community College projected attrition rates of 60 to 70 percent for Open Admissions students in the senior colleges, 70 to 80 percent for Open Admissions students in the junior colleges. Rempson considered these figures "astonishing"—and indeed they are, though not in the sense Rempson intended; for the evidence of their previous schoolwork would have argued that virtually *none* of these students could handle a full program of higher education without kinds and degrees of help beyond what CUNY has provided. Until the fall of 1972, when Manhattan and Queensborough Community Colleges wielded a small ax, no Open Admissions students were flunked out

anywhere in the City University system, and the 50 percent
or so who left during the first two years did so on their
own.

A substantial proportion of those who leave the colleges do so for economic reasons: many are from fearfully
poor families, and find $1.40 a day in carfare a heavy bur-
den to carry. But there is no question among either supporters or opponents of Open Admissions that a considerable majority of the survivors are doing badly. They are
mostly dull students, and they sit as dull students will in a
class, wrapped in an invisible blanket that protects them
from all the things they do not dare. For what the observation is worth, the black and Puerto Rican students seem
on the average more alert: the counselors' typical statement that "test scores do not really predict performance for
black students" is not just propaganda for the cause. Still,
most of the black and Puerto Rican students accepted under Open Admissions are doing badly, too.

What constitutes "success" for the Open Admissions venture is an impossible question to answer. When the doors
first opened to the freshmen of 1970, Vice-Chancellor Timothy S. Healy told *Time* magazine that if "20 percent of
these kids get a degree, that's 20 percent above zero." Recently Mrs. Jacqueline Wexler, president of Hunter College, commented that "if we can move 25 percent of these
kids it would be the greatest thing in the history of New
York." No one (except, unfortunately, the students themselves) expects Open Admissions entrants to complete their
degree work in four years: conventionally admitted freshmen at City University, and their peers in the country's
other urban colleges, average little short of three years for
an A.A. [Associate of Arts], six years for an A.B. The final
figures are thus a long time away. And it should be remem-
bered that the 75 percent who do not complete the course
are not necessarily losers. "The *institution* may want them
to get a degree," says Harry Heinemann of the cooperative
education program at LaGuardia Community, "but if they

take thirty hours and that gets them a job they like, they haven't failed—they've succeeded."

On the other hand, what defines *failure* for Open Admissions is an easy question to answer: it is a decline in the respect accorded to a diploma from a branch of City University. "If we move 60 percent of these kids through social promotion," says Mrs. Wexler, using an elementary-school term of art, "it will be a disaster for the city. Unless the city can be got to see that, we will be doing a terrible disservice."

City headquarters has begun judging the colleges by the numbers of credits Open Admission students receive—and the students themselves, of course, have been learning from the grapevine about teachers who pass everybody. With the elimination of all degree requirements other than numbers and the removal of prerequisites from all courses at places like City College, the chance to collect empty credits has been multiplied, and so has the chance to collect empty diplomas. The losers will be not only the regular students, but also that fraction of the Open Admissions students who in fact complete a valid college program at what Vice-Chancellor Hyman calls "some level of acceptability." Marvin Schick, a former Hunter political science professor who is liaison between the mayor's office and CUNY, points out that "many state universities, including some famous ones, were giving diplomas for very low qualities of work for years, and the country was none the worse for it." But the fact is that high school diplomas are being given today in New York for work below anything that would be considered acceptable outside big cities, and it is hard to see why City University will not follow the same path.

The pressures City University must resist are not just political. Open Admissions has turned most of the campuses into enclosures crowded to the limits of endurance. Four-year colleges in the State University system outside the city average about 205 "gross square feet" [GSF] per student, excluding residential space; City University four-year colleges in fall 1971 averaged 86 "gross square feet" per student. (The opening of new buildings at CCNY and Brooklyn improved this figure to 97 GSF in 1972, but better than that it will not be in this decade.) It is not uncommon to see students sitting on the floor in the hallways, getting some work done between classes; at Hunter College during class breaks the elevators are as jammed as a rush-hour subway car. The atmosphere is uncivilized, denying all those values beyond course work which a college is supposed to inculcate.

One of the greatest threats to the quality of the diplomas may come from the growth of a central City University bureaucracy that will, like all bureaucracies, seek neat answers to difficult questions. Already some of the resemblances to the Board of Education are startling and frightening. (When I called and told the secretary of a vice-chancellor that I was writing an article about Open Admissions and wished to see her boss, she said sweetly, "You want his permission to write the article?") A central task force is now at work on the problem of continuing racial imbalance among the campuses, and it will probably recommend a "comprehensive school" solution, with everyone to take the first two years at two-year colleges. "That," says Mrs. Wexler, "would *really* be the destruction of the city." But it may happen.

Stress on the Faculty

Though the numbers of able students entering the city colleges have not dropped seriously, the proportion of able students a professor encounters during his day is down considerably; and at some of the branches, notably City College, it seems possible that the tipping point has been passed. This is a grievous worry. "The performance of a given staff," says City's Abraham Mazur, "will depend on the presence of a certain number of really good students. It's happened to me—I put out more, I'm more creative, when I have really good students. We felt the difference here when the cut off dropped from 85 to 82 back in the

1950s, and now. . . . If it weren't for the Chinese we'd be in trouble already."

I can't fault the faculty for the psychological problem they obviously face [says Chancellor Kibbee]. It's much more fun to confront the student at something like your intellectual level. If I'd been a professor at CCNY for ten or fifteen years, I'd wonder whether all this was worth it. If you start at some teachers' college in western Pennsylvania and work your way up to Yale it's very different from starting at Yale and winding up at a teachers' college in western Pennsylvania—even if you get a bigger title and a bigger salary.

Even the carefully-maintained facade of official optimism about Open Admissions has developed serious cracks. Explaining the failure of his planning committee to give people anything of substance to do with the newcomers, David Newton says, "Does a college belong in the remedial business? No. But I figured we could carry it for five or ten years without seriously damaging our educational function, and by then the high schools would be repaired. . . ." Vice-Chancellor Hyman worries that "the soft areas are heavily oversubscribed, and increasingly so. Things like sociology. It seems to be an easy curriculum: people feel that all you have to be is sufficiently verbal and you can survive it." The integrity of the diploma, Hyman says, "involves reliance on the professional integrity of the professor." That's an awfully weak reed in an age when administrators demand results and so many professors have lost their nerve without losing their vanity.

"There's no real way you can maintain the standards of the diploma from this office," says Chancellor Kibbee, adding that while he would consider the graduation of 30 percent of the first Open Admissions group "a qualified success," he would then "like to make it 40 percent." To the extent that the pressure from headquarters is to give more and more credits and more and more diplomas, the deck is stacked against those in the faculties who care about what the diploma certifies. Nothing is more disturbing in this connection than CUNY's expressed desire to load the private colleges with the same problems, and the same pressures to award unearned degrees. Thus, major efforts will be made in the state legislature in the next few years to develop grant mechanisms to lure financially pressed NYU and Columbia and the city's other private colleges into taking on large numbers of unprepared students. Vice-Chancellor Timothy Healy says, "So long as Open Admissions is solely in the public sector, it will merely substitute the question of *where* did you go to college for the question of *did* you go to college." But surely the question would not arise in this form if CUNY maintained the quality of its diploma.

Yet when all one's outrage at these attitudes has been expended, it remains true that what is most objectionable in the promotion of Open Admissions is merely a natural outgrowth of the abuse of educational credentials by employers and, indeed, by the public at large. The students at LaGuardia Community College are entirely right in their argument that one does not need a college education to be a bank teller, but as the supply of college graduates increases, the banks will certainly begin to demand an A.B. from all candidates for such positions. When there was a shortage of engineers in this country, employers happily imported English "engineers" who had been through a year or two of postsecondary training—but they would not hire Americans with less than a B.S. The "nursing profession" has now succeeded in imposing an A.B. prerequisite on future nurses in New York State. Many of our best airline captains are alumni of high school and the World War II air force, but now neither the airlines nor the air force will accept for pilot training anyone who does not have a bachelor's degree. One can easily foresee a future in which policemen, factory foremen, barbers, morticians, apartment-house janitors, TV repairmen will be required to show possession of a baccalaureate.

Equality and Excellence

Despite many gloomy forecasts, America need never worry about a large class of unemployed college graduates: the system is rigged so that demand must grow to meet the available supply. What will happen to the colleges in the process is visible in the current plight of the high schools. But higher education today is intellectually defenseless against the insistence on ever-expanding enrollments, and ever-easier degrees. "The American university," Reck Niebuhr of Temple once said, "has failed to *conceptualize* its manpower function." And in the meanwhile it has become saddled with a function it cannot perform.

There are more false gods here than one can shake a stick at. Education is inherently a promoter of inequality. The musically talented and the tone deaf play the fiddle equally well in a community where there is no violin teacher; once instruction begins, a gap develops. Very nearly the only operational truth ever demonstrated in education is that something must be worth doing if the results of the work show some improvement for everybody and a widening of the gap between the best and the poorest. The better the training the more salient the revealed differences in natural ability; only academicians who live in the literature of their subject rather than in their experience could even imagine education as a promoter of equality. More strikingly for individuals than for groups (as Christopher Jencks has so wearisomely pointed out), education can open opportunities that would be closed in its absence. But its necessary social function in a complex modern society must be to raise the general floor under performance and understanding, not to reduce the distance between the floor and the ceiling.

Though I know many brilliant people I would not care to have as my doctor or my lawyer or my children's teacher, it is undoubtedly true that a unidimensional measure of academic excellence can be used to set a special, higher floor for many occupations and professions. The ardently egalitarian researchers of the Amercian Council on Education are fundamentally unconvincing: one can dismiss them with the curse that they should cross the river on a bridge designed by an engineer from an engineering school where students were admitted by lottery; and that their injuries should then be treated by a doctor from a medical school where students were admitted by lottery; and that their heirs' malpractice suit should then be tried by a lawyer from a law school where students were admitted by lottery. The problems even of affluent America are not primarily distributive—it still makes an immense, perhaps even a growing, difference who does how well a large number of highly skilled and difficult jobs. But that number is already much smaller than the number of college-trained workers, and it is surely appropriate to wonder what social function is served by maintaining high "standards" for credentials that then grant exclusive access to jobs that can be done just as well by people who have not achieved such standards.

The Open Admissions students deserve better than that: despite all the media images, they are in overwhelming proportion grave, earnest, desperately hardworking, and insecure. It is not their fault that they must make their rites of passage to adulthood in a society that values not education itself—let alone learning—but the institutional evidence that education has occurred. They are not very bright, most of them, but their perception of their social situation is correct.

No doubt college does civilize some who were merely acculturated by elementary and secondary education. Higher education for those who wish to understand better and enjoy more profoundly should always be "open," voluntary on both sides. But these are not the drives that can (or will) fill City University (or combine to finance it at a rate of nearly half a billion dollars a year). What is beating at all the universities—but especially at CUNY—is involuntary education on the tertiary level, the forced prolongation of an outworn adolescence for purposes that are quite separate from the civilizing Idea of a university.

REFORMING THE CURRICULUM [4]

Five years ago this spring [1974], Brown University, a venerable and traditionally conservative member of the prestigious Ivy League, launched a program of academic reform more radical than that attempted by any other major university. The New Curriculum, as it was called, was widely publicized and acclaimed. The Harvard *Crimson* published a long two-part report on the program, a description was included in a report of the Carnegie Commission on Higher Education, and applications from bright high school seniors flooded the admissions office.

This spring an Ad Hoc Committee to Review the Baccalaureate Degree Requirements contented itself with recommending only minor changes in the program. But in the process the committee once again raised a number of basic issues about the mission of the university, and Brown's experience since 1969 provides a classic case history of the rewards and the frustrations that accompany attempts to reform complex educational institutions.

The new curriculum was designed to allow—and to stimulate—students to take more responsibility for their own education. Therefore, the traditional academic structures were largely eliminated in an effort to make it possible for students to design a program of study that would serve their own interests and desires. Specifically, all course requirements were eliminated, and distribution requirements were jettisoned. New emphasis was given to student initiative by allowing as many independent studies as a student wished, and students were permitted to create their own courses and programs. At the same time the mandatory A, B, C grading system was eliminated, and students were allowed to take as

[4] From "Experiment With Radical Reform," by James Cass, education editor. *Saturday Review/World.* Je. 1, '74. p 49. Reprinted by permission.

many of their courses as they wished on a satisfactory/no-credit basis.

The other major element of the new curriculum was the introduction of a program called Modes of Thought courses, designed primarily to place freshmen in small, informal classes, where they would have close contact with stimulating faculty and would be introduced to the underlying concepts that relate the different areas of knowledge—in contrast to the usual freshman survey courses. Clearly, the elements of Brown's new curriculum were not new, but rarely has so dramatic an attempt been made to revolutionize the whole fabric of a university's academic life.

A Test of "Student Power"

A crucial element in Brown's experiment in radical reform was the fact that it was student-initiated and largely student-designed and that students played a major role in shepherding the new curriculum through the intricate process of faculty and administration approval. The revolution started slowly. During the 1966–67 school year, a group of students met regularly to study the history of American higher education as background for assessing their own undergraduate experiences. At first the group had in view an experimental college or a free university associated with the parent institution, but they gradually concluded that their objective should be a thorough reexamination of the entire university curriculum.

During the summer of 1967, the university provided financial support for the group to continue their studies and, the following year, set up a committee to consider their proposals. In succeeding months, as the proposals were debated, substantial numbers of students and faculty became involved in reexamining their assumptions about the nature and purpose of education. The culmination came in May 1969, when, after three days of deliberation and debate, the faculty approved fundamental changes in the university's academic life.

But as one senior, a member of the first class to enter Brown under the new curriculum, put it last spring: "The golden age that everyone perceived four years ago just hasn't materialized. It is easy to tear down structures, but the old attitudes remain."

A number of obvious reasons explain why the new curriculum never fully fulfilled its golden promise. Almost immediately after Brown's academic revolution, the university, like most other private colleges and universities, was caught in a severe financial crunch. Many of the programs initiated were never fully funded. A massive counseling program, designed to help students make the transition from high school to the new academic freedom of the university, never got off the ground. Developing Modes of Thought seminars was never made compulsory for departments, and faculty who volunteered to sponsor MOTs or independent-study projects had to do so in addition to their regular departmental teaching load—and without additional compensation. The old academic structures had been eliminated, but new structures within which fresh approaches to instruction and learning could function were never developed.

A New Set of Attitudes

The faculty, too, reflected a wide range of attitudes toward radical change in the university. Some members, including widely respected scholars, responded enthusiastically to change. Others, although welcoming the effort to reduce academic competition, felt strongly, as one department chairman put it, that the new curriculum failed "to take into account the character and traditions of the university."

But most important, perhaps, were the changing attitudes of the students who came to Brown in the seventies. Many members of the first class that entered Brown under the new curriculum caught the enthusiasm for change that had been generated on campus, and they made the most of the freedom offered them. But the following spring, Cambodia and Kent State marked the end of the euphoria of the sixties on campuses all over the country. Academic realities reasserted themselves. Satisfactory/no-credit grades posed a threat to acceptance by graduate and professional schools rather than an opportunity for intellectual exploration and self-discovery. Students became more pragmatic, accepting, career-oriented. Today only a few perceive the vision of a "golden age."

Judgments on Brown's experiment in radical educational reform range from "it's dead" to assertions that all that is necessary is a little tinkering with the new curriculum. However, it seems more accurate to say that although Brown's revolution of 1969 never fulfilled its promise, it has provided for many students a free environment for learning, rather than merely professional preparation for graduate school—and it still does so for those who desire it.

IV. THE NEW STUDENT MOOD ON CAMPUS

EDITOR'S INTRODUCTION

As a generalization it can be said that students, as a group, never quite fit their public image. Not all the students of the sixties were fire-eating radicals, and not all those of the fifties were apathetic bores. The truth is probably that the great majority of students differ relatively little from one decade to the next in basic concerns. And that applies to the students of the seventies. They are not throwbacks to the get-ahead grinds of the fifties or even to the brother-can-you-spare-a-dime scholars of the thirties, as some observers have implied. They are as socially and politically aware as students have always been. They have their favored fads and fancies. Their hair styles change, but not their basic reasons for going to college—or not going. Given the pressures of the time, they may be slightly more "adult" than their predecessors. But they are still young people in search of themselves and their careers.

Times change, however, and students react. The mood on campus changes. We are witness to such a change in mood today. Politics-as-theater is out, although Stephen Weissman argues in the first article in this section that serious politics remains very much in. Life-styles change to match realities. The social conscience of the opulent sixties gives way to the more personal demands imposed by hard times. As the third article in this section suggests, students even cohabit informally, partly as a means of delaying the financial responsibilities inherent in marriage—responsibilities less easily borne today than in the more prosperous past.

This section sketches out the basic attitudes and preoccupations of American college students today. The first article indicates that the mood shaped by the sixties remains more widespread, in its positive aspects, than most people think. The second article, from the New York *Times*, suggests a new emphasis on training, professionalism, and a revived work-ethic as dominant campus themes. The third article outlines the changing sexual mores of today's undergraduates. The section closes with a discussion of the gradual revival of fraternity-sorority life on campus, if on a somewhat altered basis from the past.

PULLING DOWN THE BARRICADES [1]

The students at the country's major universities have stopped seizing buildings and breaking windows, and the mass media are interpreting this as a retreat from social concerns and radical commitments. The president of Columbia University may have set the tone for countless commencement speeches by noting on his campus this year's "nostalgic rediscovery" of the "half-forgotten joys" and "golden optimism" of the 1950s.

Having spent the past year as a research associate at Stanford University, and after interviewing dozens of students, faculty members and administrators, I'm skeptical of these analyses. In fact, the students here maintain a high level of critical social and political consciousness, although its manifestations are less dramatic, disruptive of academic routines, and all-pervasive than they were in the days of mass mobilization. That significant minority which was more or less "radicalized" by the activism of recent years has become even more deeply committed to the struggle for major social changes. Far from being disillusioned, they are in general better organized and less millenarian, more strategy-oriented and less contaminated by the excesses of counterculture "spontaneity."

And they have been refreshed by troops from new movements, particularly women and Chicanos, whose specific

[1] From "No Retreat from Commitment," by Stephen R. Weissman, a political science research associate at Stanford University. *Nation*. 216:781-5. Je. 18, '73. Reprinted by permission.

grievances often lead to more critical social perspectives. The new campus movement uses the gains of the 1960s—the institutionalizing of a critical opposition in the educational sphere, the opportunity to relate to off-campus political groups—to involve a large minority in a multitude of social issues. Indeed, the combined number of students doing such things as investigating prison conditions and responding to prisoners' legal and educational needs, organizing support for the United Farm Workers Union in its battle with the Teamsters and growers, studying and experimenting with curricula for free schools, working for McGovern as a step toward pushing the country to the Left, and setting up a counseling center on alternative, socially relevant vocations, is probably larger than the number who sat in during 1969 and 1970.

There is, to be sure, less opportunity for casual participation, as by attending a mass rally, than there was in the apocalyptic days. There's even some breathing space for such conservative side phenomena as a minirevival of fraternities and the flowering of the Jesus movement. But the reigning ideology is liberal. Campus resocialization carries a large minority of privileged white students to Left-liberal or radical positions, either through direct involvement in issues or by a less tangible cultural osmosis. The forms of political action do challenge the system, although they are less violent than those of an earlier period.

And Stanford may not be untypical of the current situation on America's "elite" campuses, from which the movement of the 1960s sprang. It is, if anything, more "bourgeois" and "suburban" than Harvard, Columbia, Berkeley and Cornell. According to the university's placement counselors, most Stanford students are sorely tempted to spend their lives, in whatever capacity, amid the enticing and distracting lushness of Palo Alto, Los Altos Hills and Portola Valley.

No "Return of the 1950s"

On examination, the notion of a return to the 1950s seems illusory. At the end of that decade Stanford had twenty-six fraternities and an overwhelming preference for Richard Nixon as the next President of the United States. By the mid-1960s, things had changed somewhat. David Harris returned from Mississippi summer, became student union president by appealing to students in the dorms rather than those in the fraternities, and started the Resistance. In 1969–71 several hundred among Stanford's eleven thousand students were willing, at appropriate moments, to become involved in high-risk, forceful action against the university's military research and ROTC programs. Several thousand others rallied to support these demands and heard far-reaching criticisms of American society. A majority of these voted, in special referenda, for the demilitarization of the university, American withdrawal from Southeast Asia, the Panther demand for liberation of all political prisoners, and the reinstatement of radical Professor H. Bruce Franklin who was fired in a *cause célèbre* of academic freedom for such alleged incidents as encouraging students to shut down a Computation Center where a war-related program was being run off.

This year only fourteen fraternities remain; 80 percent of student voters went for George McGovern; the newly installed student government is every bit as activist and Left-leaning as its recent predecessors, although the Stanford *Daily* has acquired a less militant (but liberal) staff. The number of students enrolled in Stanford Workshops on Political and Social Issues (SWOPSI), a sort of counter-curriculum for credit which resulted from Movement agitation, has doubled in the past year. Student leaders of varying political persuasions characterize the present phase as one of "high consciousness and low mobilization." Faculty members with whom I spoke tended to agree. Assistant Professor Ward Watt, who teaches introductory biology, observed that his students are more persevering and "less distracted by mass excitation" than three years ago, but adds, "They are quite interested in social problems. I've never found as much interest in the connections between science and these other questions. I don't think there are indications that they're moving down and turning in." John Mollenkopf, an assistant professor of political science, has noted that his classes are "shot through with a large number of people who were permanently changed by antiwar stuff, the Movement, who talk of intellectual issues but are sometimes confused about current directions." In the Law School, Professor Anthony Amsterdam believes that the "marked change" in law student activism that resulted from the 1960s has persisted in this less noisy era. He detects "no decrease in social consciousness" in the last two or three years. The dean of undergraduate admissions, Fred Hargadon, flatly states that "a large majority of candidates accepted are socially conscious and concerned with issues." Although Hargadon is skeptical as to the depth of their commitment and regards the rapid succession of issues as a symptom of "media other-direction," he has become accustomed to application essays on Vietnam, racism and ecology, rather than "My Experiences Fishing With Maine Lobstermen."

Why, then, has the largest mass mobilization this year been a quiet rally of eight hundred in January [1973], following Nixon's decision to bomb for peace in North Vietnam? According to Dan Brenner, a junior who is opinions editor of the [Stanford] Daily, "Students today are less prone to go out on the Embarcadero and get arrested because they feel it is not an effective technique." Brent Appel, a former student union copresident who is in his fifth year at Stanford, explains, "The issue is what I can do. Demonstrations are not seen as viable—all has been heard before, it's not novel now, the average Middle American won't be reached. People are looking for new tactics." Past mobilizations also created an ideological momentum which was bound to undermine the logic of the initial tactics. Bob Saunders, another fifth-year student who is also an alternative vocations counselor, thinks: "People's expectations got to be higher than their tactics, which couldn't themselves change society. Even if you got the Defense Department off campus [which largely occurred], the capitalist structure and imperialism survived." Bruce Franklin, now laboring off campus as a member of the Central Committee of Venceremos, a Marxist-Leninist organization, speaks of the "apparent paradox" of "a low level of militant activity and high consciousness": "Because people have a high level of consciousness they don't see what they can do about [oppression]."

Another important factor in the subsidence of large eruptions has been the removal of draft pressures. In the context of Vietnam, conscription was more than a personal threat; it was, in Appel's phrase, "a symbol of government coercion at your back door." Radical organizers today have not found a similar crosscutting incentive for campus mobilization. Finally, the labor market and graduate school gluts have undoubtedly taken some toll of activism even at a prestige school like Stanford.

Less Romantic, More Organized

But while the shift away from mass mobilization has left some of the more casual former participants feeling frustrated, powerless, and occasionally cynical, that has not been the general reaction of those who were more deeply touched. There is widespread agreement with Appel's judgment that "the number of people who really commit a substantial part of their lives to social change is increasing." Furthermore, as *Daily* columnist Bill Evers points out, "The new New Left is more organized, less hedonistic and politically crazy. Achievement orientation has come back more and there's a more sensible time horizon." Leslie Rabine, a graduate student who has been active organizing women's groups remarks, "At the point where the Movement was generally at its height there was a lot of reliance on spontaneity. Now there's better organization, more solid ties. It's much more serious and long range." In organizing students, the new New Left has emphasized both consciousness raising and meaningful action. And it has made good use of the post-1960s educational revolution: greater openness of the campus to outside social change groups and the incorporation of a significant number of student-initiated, action-oriented courses. Here follow some examples of current activity:

Student government copresident Kevin O'Grady, a first-year medical student, headed the local McGovern campaign which involved more than four hundred people. With other McGovern workers and veterans of the Movement he formed SCOPE (Stanford Committee on Political Education) which recently presented a four-day conference focusing on domestic repression. The most prominent of eight Left-liberal and radical speakers was Daniel Ellsberg, who attracted 1,600 spectators. Ten years ago major universities did not countenance public appearances by individuals under indictment.

Through SWOPSI, a group of students is researching practical health-care alternatives for farm workers, in response to "an agricultural and economic system which values profits and productivity more than people, combined with a health-care system which creates barriers to accessibility and acceptability of health services." All research will be made available to the farm workers and their appropriate community organizations. Moreover, a number of students plan to join a larger group from Stanford which will work with the United Farm Workers this summer in their battle against the Teamster-grower alliance.

Senior Elaine Wong, who started some of the first women's study groups at Stanford, estimates that up to two hundred women are actively involved in SWOPSI and other student-initiated courses focusing on women's liberation. Women's caucuses are active in the law and medical schools as well as in some undergraduate departments. For most of the women organizers with whom I spoke, liberation goes beyond careerism to the redefinition of alienating occupations and institutions. A group of white women joined their Chicana sisters in picketing a department store which was selling Farah slacks.

Approximately fifty law students are active in prison, civil liberties and rights, or legal aid work. Fifteen under-graduates are getting a first-hand look at prison through a SWOPSI project, teaching black and Chicano studies and general education to inmates at Soledad.

One of the most important indications of deepening commitment has been the profusion of student-conceived courses on alternative vocations. Through policy research and direct practice, many students are learning about such structural experiments as free clinics and migrant labor health centers, free schools, law communes and the alterna-tive media. Synergy Center, devoted to the integration of new, socially meaningful vocations and life styles, is training twenty-five counselors through a SWOPSI course. In the academic sphere, future professors of leftist bent have formed study groups in at least the following departments: history, political science and economics.

Most of this activity is publicized in the *Daily* and has some influence on general student consciousness. For in-stance, a small demonstration against fraternity sexism is said to have dominated dinner conversations in some dorms for weeks.

Black students have always been chary of joining the white movement at Stanford. At the moment, according to black student union president Charles Ogletree, "The em-phasis is on acquiring the best resources available to achieve educational success." Former black student leader Mike Dawson, who graduated last year and now works for Stan-ford Linear Accelerator, confirms that "As of a year ago, one trend was to more interest in the classical professions and a decrease in community involvement. Earlier there was more talk of the university as a laboratory to practice skills in the community. Recently there has been less interest in political and more in cultural issues." Although there are exceptions, this seems to portray the general drift. Perhaps it is an inevitable characteristic of first-generation-in-college, upwardly mobile ethnics, but some think that rising admissions requirements for blacks and the withdrawal of the Panthers from the campuses have also played a role. The less firmly established Chicanos, who can look to the example of Cesar Chavez, have been somewhat more active.

With the end of the shattering mass mobilizations of the late 1960s, conservative groupings have picked up a bit. There has been an increase in the number of students choosing to live in fraternities, but nothing very spectacular. The principal manifestation of conservative political thought is the Radical Libertarian organization which has about sixty members. But its program, a hybrid of Milton Friedman economic liberalism and New Left antimilitarism, would give cold comfort to Richard Nixon or David Packard.

"Peace and Joy Through Jesus"

Perhaps the largest and most rapidly growing group on campus is the amorphous "Jesus movement." It is sponsored by evangelical Protestant organizations and appears to have a few hundred followers. Previously based mainly in western high schools, it ran a highly successful canvassing operation in the freshman dorms this year. The movement offers peace and joy through a personal relationship with Jesus, who is considered to be an active force shaping people's lives. It stands for many of the old tenets of fundamentalist morality but has imparted a new flexibility toward youthful indiscretions, clothing styles and even women's lib. Its characteristic activities are Bible study sessions, which have incorporated some aspects of encounter groups; joint prayer, and summer retreats. For the fairly conservative young people who embrace it (a good many are athletes), it seems to provide an antidote to competitive personal relations, self-doubt, indecision and institutional impersonality that they do not find in "good works" Christianity. Freshman Carol Sawyer expressed some themes which recurred in my conversations with Jesus people:

> I was hung up on decisions, relations with people, how I was going to change things—I haven't such control. Now that I have Christ, He guides me in my decision. No matter which way I go I don't get hung up on it. No matter where I go I have a peace about my decision. I'm less self-centered—He's helped me. I can get along better with some, have understanding and love for them, through my relation with Christ. When I came to Stanford I knew some Christians. I noticed they were like little lights—so happy, joyful, had a peace, weren't upset. I found out some even prayed for me when I blew an exam or my mom was mad at me. They related to me on a very personal, interested basis. The Lord has special timing for me. They had something. I wanted their peace and joy.

However inwardly turning and apolitical, the Jesus movement is no return to the values of the 1950s. It seems more connected to the social strains that gave rise to the counterculture of the 1960s. Its followers are critical of the competitive insecurity and empty materialism of American life, and disillusioned by the failure of national power, science and sometimes the student movement to solve these problems. Many have come to the Jesus movement after experiences with drugs or Eastern religions.

Needless to say, college students of the industrialized Western nations can never by themselves be a decisive revolutionary force. But, as events in France and the United States have shown, they can be the cutting edge of a troubled society. If their movements are marked by the impermanence of their educational experience, it is also true that the young, by their self-definitions, have shaped "political generations." (Nearly all the Stanford student leaders of the 1960s are now in "alternative vocations" which permit them to continue their work for political change.) Kenneth Keniston and others have shown that the contradictions of our society have produced large numbers of "committed" or "alienated" young people who come together in many of our best universities. As a result of the 1960s, these universities are even more open to political thought and practice than they were in the 1950s. While the forms of involvement have responded to changing external conditions, the critical thrust seems firmly established.

RETURN OF THE WORK ETHIC [2]

College students around the country are changing their tastes in studies away from many of the abstract and theoretical courses that were popular during the 1960s and toward studies that teach "hard" knowledge or that lead to professional training and a comfortable career.

Some college deans are calling it "the new vocationalism," while Dean Stephen Trachtenberg of Boston University called it a search for a combination of "wisdom and prosperity."

Whatever the name, a survey by campus correspondents of the New York *Times* reveals, it boils down to a shift toward the concrete in college studies.

On campuses from coast to coast, academic deans and advisers are finding that students this fall [1973] are swelling the enrollments in premed, prelaw, business, nursing, agriculture and the newly developing health-sciences and handicapped-training courses.

In most cases, students were frank to point out that the jobs and security beckoning at the end of a long and arduous professional training were a prime reason for their choices.

"The liberal arts universities are becoming preprofessional or pretechnical schools," said Robert J. Kiely, Harvard's associate dean of the faculty for undergraduate education. He noted "tremendous increases in concentration in biochemistry and biology," which are standard premedical courses.

"People are very, very concerned about jobs," he added.

[2] From " 'New Vocationalism' Now Campus Vogue," by Iver Peterson, staff reporter. New York *Times*. p 19. D. 25, '73. © 1973 by The New York Times Company. Reprinted by permission.

At the University of California at Los Angeles, the number of students majoring in biology has doubled in the last two years. At Northwestern, half of the undergraduates say they are premed.

Freshman chemistry has almost doubled its enrollment at the University of California at Berkeley since 1968, and students are having to share scarce laboratory space. At Stanford ten years ago, history, political science and English were the most heavily subscribed courses; today, psychology, biology and human biology are most popular.

The University of Minnesota, meanwhile, recently surveyed enrollments at its various campuses and found "significant increases in the professional and vocationally oriented colleges and campuses," while enrollments at the liberal arts-oriented Morris campus seemed to be "undergoing a larger enrollment decline than was expected," the university said.

"Students are saying, 'I need some training for a particular job, and I want this college to give it to me,' " William Connellan, assistant to the president at Oakland University commented.

While it must be noted that no two students, colleges or courses are alike, the *Times* survey also revealed these broad trends:

☐ Ecology courses, once a "hot" topic, have declined in enrollment at many campuses, especially those in urban areas, where interest in the natural sciences and biomedical sciences have drawn students away. Rural campuses reported that ecology was still popular, however.

☐ Far Eastern and occult religions which got an assist from rock groups, gurus and truth-seekers from Beverly Hills in the late 1960s, are fading. Interest in them has been replaced by religious questions closer to home—Jewish and Christian studies, in particular.

☐ Radical courses that explored and often advocated radical themes, which grew rapidly during the years of student activism, are also declining in popularity. At Boston University, a student-taught "radical critique" course that once flourished as an example of students seeking control of the curriculum is now "withering on the vine," according to a faculty adviser there.

☐ Sociology, or social relations as it is sometimes known, was a big attraction a decade ago but, students reported, it has become tainted by an association with social engineering and behavior control, and has suffered some loss in popularity.

Engineering in Comeback

Course choices are routinely influenced by the job market in various fields, as the slump in engineering enrollments following a decline in the aerospace industry two or three years ago showed. Now engineering is making a comeback.

Teaching courses are also showing declining registration as primary and secondary school enrollments level off and a surplus of teachers has developed. But some teaching fields are still understaffed—communicative disorders, teaching the handicapped and special therapy, for example—and these areas are being rapidly developed on many campuses.

Current events also have their effect. China is a hot topic of study, and, at Berkeley, a course on Chile doubled its enrollment after the military coup there.

Student views on why they chose a certain major varied widely, of course, from "money" to "it's a good conversational item." But deans and advisers, as well as a number of students, made plain that the security a professional career offered was a greater consideration today than it was five years ago.

"I think green is green," David Bradt, a freshman at Northwestern said candidly, "and a person must have a certain amount of financial basis to start with."

Jeff Blutstein, a prelaw student at Hampshire College in Amherst, Massachusetts, put a countercultural spin on the

old success drive in his reasons for wanting to follow his
father into the insurance business:

"If I were a poet, I'd starve," he said, "but fortunately
I'm not. I want to make money so I can smoke good pot,
have a nice car, and wear good clothes. I want to wear $200
suits, which is the proper uniform for a life insurance agent
anyway."

A professional career also appears to hold two other
qualities that may indicate that today's college students are
not simply apathetic throwbacks to the career-conscious
fifties. A number of students specified that a professional
career appeared to be the only way to be self-employed, to
avoid "being a cog in some machine."

Women and minority students in particular saw an obligation—matched by newly opening opportunities—to apply
their skills in causes helpful to themselves as well as to their
own kind.

"Premed is what's happening if you can manage it," a
freshman at the predominantly black Fisk University in
Nashville said. "First, we never will have enough black doctors if some of us don't stop rapping so much about conditions and doing nothing about them, and second, you just
can't escape the fact that there's some money involved—and
you've got to have capital to survive in America.

The popularity of the country's two blue-chip professions, medicine and law, has already brought blizzards of
applications to law and medical schools for tightly limited
space.

In 1963, for example, 17,668 students mailed 70,000 applications for 8,842 available medical school places. This
school year, 37,000 students will fill out 250,000 applications
for 13,500 spaces, according to the Association of American
Medical Schools, which estimates that three quarters of the
applicants are qualified to take the training.

A growing number of disappointed applicants, therefore,
are flying off to European medical schools where local governments, jealous of the heavy subsidies necessary for all

medical training, have begun adopting restrictions against "foreign"—meaning American—applicants.

Greater Maturity Found

Some professors and deans who were interviewed recently cautioned against anyone drawing the conclusion that today's students are nothing more than flinty-hearted careerists, however.

A lot of them, it was said, have simply learned a thing or two about the illusions of the recent past when the "greening" of the youth culture meant anything but money.

Dean Trachtenberg of Boston University saw a "greater maturity" among middle-class students in the realization "that once you graduate you're going to have to feed yourself.

"Take the back-to-the-earth movement of the last few years," Dr. Trachtenberg went on. "The best way to deal with illusions is to live them out, I've always thought, and the best thing that kids learned on farms was that the earth was not cooperative in letting you do your own thing. If you don't pick that tomato, it's going to rot.

"So a kid who earlier thought he was going to spend his life in a semirural environment now may say it might be a good idea to take some courses in forestry to find out what really works."

The dean also cited a trend toward double majors—chemistry and philosophy, for example—that he called, with his taste for alliteration, "a marriage of passion and precision."

Although they concede it is not a sound practice to try to psychoanalyze a generation of students on the basis of the courses they choose, some educators suggest that new tastes in studies may reflect an evolving view of the world.

The fascination with politics, dialectics, movements—"the system"—that characterized much of the 1960s may be fading, they suggest, in favor of a concern about the self and for one's place in the world and its history.

This may be why, according to some teachers, interest in

the solid, traditional and "basic" humanities—the classics, Shakespeare, philosophy—is still strong while courses that are politicized, highly abstract or theoretical about social issues are less popular.

Academic deans at some large state universities feel another spur toward stressing the practical in their course offerings: As the costs of education continue to mount, and as college enrollments level off, state legislatures are urging that what money there is be devoted to studies that turn out men and women able to do the jobs that most need to be done.

The Regents of the University of Minnesota, for example, are urging that such courses as engineering, agriculture, biological sciences, veterinary medicine and the health sciences be emphasized on state campuses.

Grand Valley State College in Allendale, Michigan, had some trouble getting its appropriation through the legislature recently when the lawmakers began questioning the value of some of the college's experimental courses, such as Organic Homesteading, or one on weaving—A study of Textile Interlacements—each for five credits.

The final affront may have come when one student got eighteen credits for starting a petition drive to roll back salary increases for the legislators. It failed.

A NEW SEXUAL ETHIC? [3]

The past one and a half decades have seen a number of research reports on what might be called "students and the college experience." Much of the research has pointed out the importance of a student's interaction with his or her peers. However, very little of it has dealt in any depth with students' relationships with the opposite sex. Considering the emphasis placed on dating and heterosexual activity at

[3] From "College Student Cohabitation," by James L. Morrison, associate professor of education, University of North Carolina, and Scott Anderson, graduate student at Pennsylvania State University. *Education Digest*. 39:57-9. My. '74. Condensed from *College Student Journal*. 7:14-19. N.-D. '73. Reprinted by permission.

this point in their lives, it would seem reasonable to assume that some of the most influential experiences during these years are the relationships students have with members of the opposite sex.

An increasing phenomenon among college students is the "consensual union," also known as "nonlegal voluntary marriage," "living together," or "cohabitation." Not only may cohabitation be an important part of the collegiate experience, it may also be a process which has societal implications. The experience may have an influence on the larger society as well as the college environment, particularly as it might influence the nature of heterosexual interaction off campus or even the marital relationship. Unfortunately, it seems to be almost ignored in professional literature.

If one of the functions of the college is to assist young people to adequately fulfill their future roles, then cohabitation and its effect on personal growth and development is an area that can hardly be ignored.

Many sociologists and professionals in the field of marriage and the family argue that the institution of marriage in the United States is changing. Many have predicted a general change in patterns of sexual behavior. Of course, cohabitation may be a result of more than changing sexual attitudes to match behavior; it may also indicate something about marriage as youth see it. They have come of age in a society where the divorce rate is tremendous and the frequency of unhappy marriages must be even higher.

Other factors may be involved. Students today face a job market that offers little promise and rising expenses. Housing, food, and medical bills all represent threatening expenses to the newly married couple with limited job opportunities. Marriage, and the commitment implicit in it, may be regarded as too big a step for many youth faced with these pressures.

Views toward traditional marriage appear to be changing, perhaps due in part to the efforts of women's liberation. As a consequence, many college women are increasingly

considering the possibilities of a career or profession in their
own right, and becoming increasingly hesitant to settle down
in the well-known role of the young wife putting her husband through school.

The above factors, and the availablity of safe, convenient
contraceptives, along with more liberalized housing policies
on campus, may be responsible for the increasing frequency
of cohabitation that we are witnessing.

Research Results

Given our conception of cohabitation, we conducted a
number of informal interviews from summer 1971 through
winter 1972 to obtain a sense of the nature and pattern of
cohabiting relationships. We selected a sample of under-
thirty students who would speak freely regarding a cohabiting relationship in which they participated. From these interviews, it was possible to construct a pattern of behavior.

Initiation. No clearly distinguishable point in time may
be cited for the initiation of cohabitation. All of our respondents had been involved in their relationship for some
time before they actually "moved in."

Exclusivity. Exclusivity seems to develop informally and
is maintained as an expectation. As the couple sees more
and more of each other, they tend to see less and less of other
people. Several respondents indicated that an important
characteristic of the cohabiting relationship was "openness"
—they could *try* other people if they wanted to. However,
many acknowledged that they would feel hurt, surprised, or
angry if their partner took advantage of this openness, and
would probably "retaliate" by initiating another relationship.

"Moving In." If the male has an apartment, they begin
to spend more time there. The female may have stayed over
several weekends by this time, and probably has some be-
longings there. As time goes on, the female spends more and
more time there, and her possessions begin to accumulate.
Both continue to feel that having two residences is desirable.

Eventually she sleeps there seven nights a week, takes her meals there, and keeps her "everyday things" there. At this point she is, in effect, living with the male in "his" apartment. If there are other roommates, her status is probably well established with them.

Often in the "moving in" stage, no considered decision of whether to live together or not is made. It appears to be a gradual transition. A cohabitation decision may not be made until the end of the school year when living arrangements for the next year are being made.

The Ongoing Relationship. The couple may live together sharing *one* residence. This brings a "publicness" to the relationship. In our sample, about half of the couples separated, one-third married, and the remainder still cohabitate. Those who continue to cohabitate fill roles much like husband and wife.

Terminating the Cohabiting Relationship. In many ways this is much like separation or divorce in a marital relationship. Property must be divided, and other "moving out" problems handled. Each member must deal with any resultant emotional trauma. After being "out of circulation" for an extended period of time, cohabitors must establish new contacts, and begin to restructure their interpersonal world.

One major difference between cohabitation and marriage may be in terms of the pretermination process. In marriage the attitude often is one of trying to work out problems because "we're *stuck* with each other." However, one of the major features of cohabitation is mobility out of the relationship. The attitude, expressed or unexpressed, of the participants, in case of problems, is often "it's good we didn't get married—see what happened!" In cohabiting relationships, parents seldom encourage the couple to solve their problems.

Almost immediately at the onset of a problem, the couple interprets this as being "the end." Often the suggestion will be made to "see other people" for a while. The cohabiting relationship usually ends shortly after such action.

An Emerging Pattern

The exploratory study reported in this essay has enabled us to identify a pattern of consensual unions. It appears that cohabitation is becoming an accepted and not unusual type of relationship among college students. The openness of the respondents as well as the number of respondents who reported knowing other cohabiting couples support this conclusion.

The cohabiting relationship appears to fulfill a number of interpersonal needs of college students, e.g., the need for a positive self-concept vis-à-vis heterosexual encounters, the security of a relatively stable intimate relationship, and convenient interaction with the opposite sex. Thus, professional staffs have a responsibility to assist students who desire cohabiting relationships in developing more self-awareness of the implications and obligations of cohabitation.

Although counseling and student personnel staffs may assist individual students in such understandings, particularly when problems of emotional stability arise, the inclusion of a section on cohabitation in traditional marriage/ family courses could be very helpful. If cohabiting relationships are indeed increasing on our nation's campuses, it is imperative that educators respond in such a way that "education" in the sense of self-awareness and understanding is increased.

HAZING NO, COMMUNITY SERVICE YES [4]

When Tony Donadio enrolled in Ohio State University . . . he was adamant against joining a fraternity because he regarded the organizations as "petty."

---

[4] From "Fraternities Reviving on a Serious Note," by Edward B. Fiske, staff reporter. New York *Times.* p 1+. D. 1, '74. © 1974 by The New York Times Company. Reprinted by permission.

... [Four years later] he celebrated Ohio State's 12-10 football victory over the University of Michigan at a beer party with his fellow members of the Sigma Chi.

"A lot of people cut fraternities down without really experiencing them," he explained.

Mr. Donadio's new attitude is shared by an increasing number of college students, and the result is that fraternities and sororities, which fell on hard times during the social activism of the 1960s, are enjoying a resurgence on many campuses.

Like the students, though, the organizations are different from those of a decade ago.

A New York *Times* survey of a dozen campuses from the University of Massachusetts in Amherst to Stanford University in Palo Alto, California, found that fraternity and sorority life is now marked by more academic seriousness and even social consciousness.

Members today give less heed than previous generations to secret rituals and handshakes, and the sort of hazing that resulted in the death of a freshman at Monmouth College in New Jersey is virtually unheard of. "There's not much nonsense going on any more," said Derry Kelly, a member of the Sigma Kappa sorority at the University of Kansas. "Houses that do hazing have trouble getting people to join."

The decline of fraternities and sororities started in the mid-1960s when students began to question the relevance of the societies to social issues and to seek new and less restrictive styles of living. Membership declined, and many chapters were forced out of existence.

"Our losses were part of the nationwide trend to question anything 'establishment,' " said Lewis Gregory, vice president of the Interfraternity Council at Kansas.

On most campuses the low point came in 1971. At the University of Michigan, for instance, the number of new members in fraternities has increased from 231 in 1971 to 435 last year [1973].

Evidence of Revival

Five new fraternities have been established at the University of California at Berkeley in the last four years, while at Duke University the percentage of undergraduate men in fraternities increased from 30 percent in 1969 to 43 percent... [in 1974]. Sorority membership has followed a similar pattern.

At the University of Kansas, fraternities and sororities report a 10 percent increase in membership over the last year. "My house has added two rooms and we finished a couple of others since last April," said Woody Grutsmacher, a business major and member of Beta Theta Pi.

Members of the organizations and university officials attributed the trend to a decline in social activism, the new academic seriousness engendered in part by the job market and what is often described as the general "return to normalcy" that marks most aspects of college life these days.

"Students are more group-oriented than a few years ago," said Cathy Gullickson, adviser to sororities at Michigan. "Independence is a little less important now."

Asked about their reasons for joining fraternities, students generally responded with terms such as "security" or "close personal relationships."

"Before I came to Duke I thought fraternities stifled a person's individuality," said Ted Stavish, a freshman at Duke University. "I thought they were sort of plastic, but as I've had contacts with frat-men it seems that there is something enlightening about a frat as far as opening someone's personality, simply because you have the security of the brotherhood."

Others cite practical reasons. Jo Williams, a member of the off-campus housing staff at Michigan, said that living and eating at a fraternity house is "a better bargain" than the alternatives. Richard Pilgrim, a student at Colorado State University, said that he joined the Alpha Gamma Rho chapter in part because "I couldn't have a water bed in the dorm."

Still another factor is the changing campus climate. "People are more passive toward fraternities than they were a few years ago," said Mr. Grutsmacher. "Not everyone is agreeing with fraternities, but they're not attacking them either."

If student attitudes have changed, so have the purposes and styles of the fraternities and sororities. Many members report, for instance, that they are now more in tune with the general academic purposes of the institutions.

"You don't see people in the house on a Saturday morning sitting around watching television with beer bottles," said Michael Macera, a member of Phi Gamma Delta at Cornell University. "They're studying."

The social consciousness of the last decade has also apparently had some effect on fraternity and sorority life. The Interfraternity Council at Kansas, for instance, has conducted two food drives to help needly persons, and sororities there have held seminars on issues raised by the women's liberation movement.

Pam Horne, assistant to the dean of women, said that sororities now seek "to educate members about what kind of insurance to buy, not simply how to buy a linen trousseau."

Changing social attitudes have caused some fraternities to become coed—Stanford has three and Cornell one—and many are loosening up or even abandoning such practices as parietal hours, house mothers and restrictions on allowing women above the first floor.

Returning alumni may still value traditions such as secret rituals and handshakes, but members themselves are apparently giving them little heed. "The traditions are demonstrated to the pledges as part of their training and initiation," said James Myerson, vice president of Kappa Alpha at Stanford. "But formalized use of them has in large part fallen into decay because people at Stanford just don't think it's relevant any more."

This is especially true of hazing activities that attracted

national attention ... [in November 1974] when William Flowers, a freshman initiate to the Zeta Beta Tau fraternity at Monmouth College, was suffocated when sand fell into a "grave" that he was forced to dig as part of his initiation.

Many states, including California and Texas, have adopted laws banning initiation rituals that are dangerous or "degrading," and numerous college administrations have issued similar regulations. ... After an initiate to one fraternity was branded on the forearm with the letters of his house, the Interfraternity Council at Cornell established strict guidelines forbidding "any physically or psychologically harmful or humiliating activities."

Hazing Rituals in Decline

The survey revealed that many fraternities still require pledges to do chores around the house or put them through physical tests such as pushups. Some still force pledges to go long periods without sleep or take them to remote locations and make them find their way back.

At the University of Texas, despite university rules forbidding such practices, pledges are reportedly routinely blindfolded and subjected to electric shocks with cattle prods.

By and large, however, the changes of the 1960s led to the virtual elimination of dangerous or physically abusive activities. "Brothers don't feel like it's necessary to engage in this sort of activity," said Rick Wagoner, president of the Delta Tau Delta chapter at Duke. "They want more of a friendship relationship."

Some see the decline as simply pragmatic. "I know six pledges in my house who will depledge if there's malicious hazing," said Daniel Janal, a nineteen-year-old member of the Theta Chi chapter at Northwestern University.

One exception to the general trend on some campuses is black fraternities, which are often heavily involved in social issues but which also continue to value secret rituals and other traditions that their white counterparts have abandoned.

At Michigan, for instance, pledges to black fraternities go through a week-long initiation that includes doing menial jobs and carrying the organization's symbol. These activities are rarely public. "You won't see any black Greeks digging holes or climbing trees or spraying buildings with purple and gold spray paint," said one black student.

Fraternities and sororities continue to be criticized for the reasons that they always have been. Lawrence R. Gottlob, a freshman at Cornell, for instance, spoke of the artificiality of fraternity life. "I can't see identifying with people just because I live with them," he said.

Some criticize the fact that many fraternities have been unable to absorb many blacks, but others say that this is not entirely their fault. "There are no written or unwritten laws about who can apply," said Frank Bell, a member of Alpha Phi Alpha, a black fraternity at Kansas. "The white Greek system is simply after different things than we are."

V. FACULTY AND ADMINISTRATORS

EDITOR'S INTRODUCTION

The final section of this compilation discusses the problems, prospects and outlook of the men and women with whom, more than anyone else, the future of higher education in America resides—the teachers and administrators of the nation's colleges. They are long-suffering, and today they are bearing the brunt of the financial crisis afflicting all institutions of higher learning. But they are resilient and ready to carry out—sometimes with tongue in cheek—their prescriptions for a better tomorrow. The four articles in this section are indicative of their unflagging optimism and dedication.

In the first article, the president of one of the nation's largest universities explains why the future of higher education still rests firmly in the hands of the faculty and the administration. The second article, from *Daedalus,* points up the need for alternate models for academic success so that a *major* goal in higher education will be excellence in teaching, rather than scholarly research, which studies show only 20 percent of all faculty devote their time to with any regularity.

The third article describes the renewed debate over the virtues and vices of academic tenure at a time of financial insecurity for all colleges and their faculties. The growing trend toward the unionization of faculties may yet constitute one of the hottest issues in higher education in the seventies. The last article, by a professor emeritus of higher education at New York University, is a call for change and for a new direction generally among the nation's colleges. The time has come, the author suggests, for colleges to stop waiting for society to change before changing themselves. A better world depends on their ability to take the lead.

AUTHORITY'S THIN RED LINE [1]

Today our publicly supported institutions of higher learning operate under a thick web of constraints and controls foreign to their earlier experience. Simply to list some of these new constraints is to suggest the range and variety of unfamiliar intrusions into the internal life of the university.

☐ Our systems for record-keeping—whether in personnel matters, the handling of radioactive waste, the policing of human subject research, or the accounting for faculty time on federal agency research projects—are increasingly dictated by various federal agencies.

☐ State civil service laws and agencies create a special group—the civil service—with its own distinct salary, leave, and retirement subsystem.

☐ The architectural design, financing, and bidding of new buildings and the renovation of old buildings on campus is likely to be a bureaucratic obstacle course.

☐ Personnel controversies that were once resolved intramurally now move almost inexorably into a maze of commissions and courts, with the hapless institution sometimes caught in conflicting, even competing, jurisdictions.

☐ Entirely new legislation, such as the Occupational Safety and Health Act, imposes new restrictions along with the burden of added costs.

☐ Specialized accrediting agencies nibble critically at the university, and with the best of intentions "cannibalize" the university.

☐ Finally—as if to usher in 1984—universities, and even groupings of universities, are consolidated under a state

[1] From "What's Left on Campus to Govern?" address by Harold L. Enarson, president, Ohio State University, delivered to the American Association for Higher Education, Chicago, Illinois, March 11, 1974. *Vital Speeches of the Day.* 40:396-8. Ap. 15, '74. Reprinted by permission.

superboard while state coordinating boards are transmuted into centralized control systems.

Thus do controls and constraints, rules and regulations and procedures descend upon the once autonomous university.

We in the university world have watched this accumulation of external authority over the life of the university in moods ranging from vague disquiet to near despair. Recently we have witnessed an acceleration in the imposition of external controls. All this has created a literature that is rich with the language of lamentation. We speak sadly of outside *intervention,* of *intrusions* into internal affairs, of the *erosion* of autonomy, of the *homogenization* of higher education, of the *excesses* of centralization. We lay full claim to the pejorative phrase, and saturate our lamentations with emotion-riddled words such as *red tape, bureaucracy, politicization,* and the like. In short, most of us bring to the new scene the fine discrimination and objectivity the Chicago *Tribune* brought to the role of the federal government. The "burocracy" that Colonel McCormick made famous now threatens to engulf us—and we do not like it one bit!

In all this, clarity of thought would be served if we were to distinguish between the rhetoric of debate and political squabble on the one hand and the reality of substantive issues on the other hand. It may be good debating tactics for universities to talk of *state bureaucrats,* just as it is good tactics for state system people to talk about institutional *insularity, narrow local perspectives,* and the like. But such rhetoric does not help us to grapple thoughtfully with immensely difficult issues.

No state-supported institution anywhere exists apart from the state which created it and whose public interest it exists to serve. By the same token, no state coordinating agency, or any other agency of government for that matter, serves the great goals of efficiency, economy, and accountability unless it has a sophisticated and sensitive grasp of the transcendent importance of quality education, in all its rich and varied meanings.

We should expect that the individual university would have legitimate concerns about the kinds of intervention it experiences at the hands of external authority. But the state agency overseeing higher education also has equally legitimate concerns. Its public charge generally includes the wise use of resources, improved delivery of educational services to neglected constituencies and communities, the fair pricing of education, and the balanced development of all the constituent units that make up a state system. Both the university and the state system agency are accountable to the public through their elected representatives. If the state agency "intrudes" in institutional affairs, as it frequently does, it is also true that the university may "intrude" in the domain of the state agency by actions that conflict with public obligations imposed on the state agency. Put simply, any unbridled provincialism on the part of the university is as threatening to the public interest as is the desire of state agencies to police universities for the sake of control itself.

Plainly the task ahead is to develop consultative relationships that bring the legitimate concerns of the individual institutions and the legitimate concerns of state agencies into shared perspectives. Warfare is too costly. Moreover, in most states both the universities and the state higher education agency share—at the deepest level of conviction—those multiple goals symbolized by words such as *equity, efficiency, economy, excellence, pluralism, diversity,* and the like. Our conflicts—intense and passionate as they seem—are hardly civil wars. Rather they are lover's quarrels by persons who see many things differently but who unite in strong conviction that the higher learning is our mutual concern and responsibility. Put still another way, some state control of public higher education is inescapable just as some substantial degree of institutional independence is indispensable. Our collective task is to make a planned "mesh of things."

Wars of maneuver are poor substitutes for responsible, creative statecraft.

Our would-be controllers need to take to heart our lectures on the tyranny of excessive centralization and thoughtless intrusion. But those of us serving in the universities need to take to heart the admonition that we cease our lamentations and take a firmer hand in attacking those matters that are unmistakably within our direct responsibility.

We ask ourselves, "What is left on campus to govern?" almost as if to invite a cynical response. In moods of exhaustion, a president is tempted to say that he is left with all the distasteful tasks of governance: to divide a starvation budget equitably, to pacify a restless student body, to telephone the mayor or governor or National Guard to quell the streakers, to mediate intramural controversies, and to put a fair face on the disaster of a losing athletic team. However, as John Gardner has so often emphasized, these large systems within which we spend our working lives contain much more elbow room for personal initiative than we dare admit, especially to ourselves.

So what's left to govern? *Just about everything.*

☐ The lump sum appropriation is fairly common; we have the necessary legal freedom to alter priorities in the division of resources.

☐ Faculty and deans and vice presidents are not hired or fired by superboards; this is our sweet privilege.

☐ The humane and efficient management of our dormitory systems is our task alone; no superboard in its right mind would have it otherwise.

☐ The initiative for seeking research grants, foundation largess, and private fund raising is exclusively ours.

☐ The demotion of losing coaches is everyone's interest but the exclusive burden of the president and/or the trustees.

☐ The organization of curricula and of courses of instruction is still our domain, as are methods of instruction and measures of student performance.

☐ We are free to reorganize our administrative structure, consolidate departments, create centers and institutes, pioneer in interdisciplinary ventures, and join in interinstitutional cooperative ventures.

☐ As for the tenure system, this briar patch is ours to enjoy or to modify as we wish.

What else is in our domain? Well, we are free to revitalize liberal education, shorten the curricula, revise subject matter requirements, and even to alter drastically the internal system of governance. We are free—thankfully—to choose the text books, the library materials, and the laboratory equipment we desire; free to alter the standard tests used for admission to professional schools; free to open classes in the evening; free to combat excesses of specialization; and free to run bars, restaurants, bookstores, art galleries, sports programs, alumni tours, overseas excursions, and all those other good things.

Perhaps we have more freedom, even with all the constraints, than we have the talent, courage, and imagination to exercise.

We are free to enforce the "no-smoking" signs in the classroom, to require full work for full pay, to equalize teaching loads, to police the manifest abuses of our grading systems, to improve space utilization by using late afternoon hours for instruction, to recruit minorities (at least for the present), and even to expel star athletes who flunk Physical Education 101.

So what else is left to govern? Only educational policy in virtually every aspect—that's all.

☐ We can despair in the face of the dreary statistics on the new depression in higher education, or we can change those educational policies and practices which deny working people of all ages equal access to educational opportunity and deny ourselves the market that we need to sustain enrollments.

☐ We can deplore the current emphasis on career training as the triumph of mere vocationalism, or we can fashion much improved counseling services along with planned work-study experiences. There is simply no good reason why the world of work and the world of formal classroom instruction cannot be melded in creative ways which permit the student to test job interests while experiencing the relevance, or lack of relevance, of formal classroom instruction.

☐ We can limp along with the present system of requirements for a baccalaureate degree, or we can critically examine our systems—more likely "non-systems"—and find ways to save everyone's time. There is something terribly wrong when a typical student requires four and one half years to complete a standard four-year program. Yet this wasteful stretch-out is now generally the common experience.

☐ We can cherish our few remaining overseas projects, lament the nation's new isolationism, deplore the fading interest of the foundations and the federal government in promoting an international dimension, or we can redefine our academic requirements to include a far more vivid sense of the diversity of world cultures and of our national dependence. The familiar incantations in defense of a foreign language requirement intone the symbols rather than the substance of cross-cultural understanding.

☐ We can be timorous in the face of collapsing standards and intellectual sloth, or we can insist that the fifty-minute classroom hour require intellectual rigor from teacher and student alike; that the grading system be fair and equitable; that the syllabus be coherent and relevant—and that it be honored; and that the teaching-learning enterprise be infused throughout with an insistence on high quality performance.

Let's face it—the agenda is crowded with tasks that are solely within the competence and concern of the individual college or university. In these great domains no state agencies constrain us, intrude upon us, or dictate to us.

It was Sartre who insisted that free men are "condemned to freedom." So it is with our colleges and universities. We are condemned to much more choice than we are prepared to acknowledge, let alone to face. It is much easier to rail at the insensitivity of "that world out there"—the governors, legislators, state bureaucracies, and an "indifferent public"— than it is to face up to the burden of choice.

But you ask, "whose choice?" And there is the rub! Is educational change the inescapable responsibility of the administration, with the faculty in an advice and consent and support role? Or is that collective entity, the faculty, finally responsible for educational policy, with the administration in a supporting role? As things now stand, one wonders who in the university is accountable for what.

As is well known, faculty and administration stereotype one another, each imputing to the other more authority and less wisdom than in truth exists. The result is that most changes are "at the margins." Change does come, but it comes slowly, haltingly, clumsily. Much of the time our universities are in a state of "dynamic immobility" (a phrase borrowed from the rector of a Latin American university). It is not that we are static—far from it. There are powerful forces at work, but these invite resistance from equally powerful countervailing forces: thus we are *dynamic* and *immobile*.

All this makes for easy evasion of responsibility. There is always a "they" standing between us and the changes we most want to make. In the last analysis, there may be no ideal distribution of power and influence and responsibility within a university, but only makeshift accommodation in the context of interests forever in conflict.

And yet, there are some old truths which deserve a reaffirmation. The complications in governance that so frustrate the administrator and baffle the outside observer grow out of a very special, little understood aspect of teaching.

Faculties are like policemen on the beat—admittedly an observation destined to antagonize both tribal groups. Both are "reverse discretion" hierarchies. In the typical bureaucracy, organization is hierarchal; policy is developed at the top and refined at each level as it moves downward to the imposition of a control or the delivery of a service. But cops and professors enjoy an extraordinary wide range of discretion precisely at that point where the control and/or service is delivered. Perhaps this is why both groups are skeptical, if not openly contemptuous, of headquarter's supervision and control. So too, this is why in the special world of the university no basic reform or change is possible without faculty support and understanding.

I realize that exhortation went out of style with Teddy Roosevelt. So if this is exhortation, make the most of it. The superboards won't destroy higher education; the Congress of the United States won't save it; and national blue-ribbon commissions won't chart our destinies. Change is now the most stable element of our times and alienation is its deadly companion. . . . The machinery for participation—for governance if you will—exists today on the North American campus. What does not exist is the willingness of enough persons who care—and who, caring, are willing to work for their convictions.

ACCENT ON TEACHING [2]

Within any educational system are basic forces which shape its response to external pressures. Whether they be a surfeit or paucity of funds, a baby boom or bust—in short, whether one looks back on the sixties or ahead to the coming decade—these forces are present and change slowly. If one wishes to analyze correctly the problems of higher education

[2] From "Thinking About Faculty," by Donald Light, Jr., assistant professor of sociology, Princeton University. *Daedalus.* 103:258-63. Fall '74. Reprinted by permission of *Daedalus,* Journal of the American Academy of Arts and Sciences, Boston, Massachusetts. Fall 1974, *American Higher Education: Toward an Uncertain Future.*

today and design policies that will work, one must understand these forces well.

Perhaps the greatest shaper of higher education is the faculty, not as a vague collection of diverse individuals, but as a cluster of professions with a certain structure and certain values. If it is disheartening to see most institutions abandon their distinctiveness to imitate the few which are said to be outstanding, if one worries about what is lost when over one quarter of all students attend institutions of over twenty thousand and one half attend schools of ten thousand or more, if the insistence that all academic subjects be treated as equally worthy and nonacademic subjects as unworthy seems wrong, if one finds universities responding to social needs in a way that serves professional reputations more than the needy, if one wonders why interdisciplinary programs are so hard to launch, then one wants to know more about the structure of the academic professions.

There are some common beliefs which start us on the wrong track. One is the functional integration of teaching and research—the assumption that each enhances the other. This assertion ignores an impressive amount of evidence to the contrary. If research-scholars teach better, it is due to their being smarter and more energetic rather than to their doing research. While much depends on what kind of research is being done and what courses are being taught, as well as who the individual is, most faculty feel they have two jobs competing for their time. This is particularly true outside the humanities. But the belief survives empirical refutation (a nice irony in itself), because it helps to integrate conflicting elements in the university and keeps faculty from being aware of these conflicts.

Another belief centers on the idea of a single academic profession. This term suggests that all faculty are of a kind, when in fact they differ in important ways. These differences become more clear, as does the relation between teaching and research, if the character of "the academic profession" is understood.

The Structure of the Academic Professions

A profession is a special kind of occupation which gains exclusive control over a prestigious body of esoteric knowledge. It is allowed to recruit, train, and license its members in return for promising to work honestly in the best interests of its clients. If this definition is accurate, then there is no single academic profession. Rather, there are academic professions, because the knowledge base for each profession is its discipline. To regard all kinds of faculty as members of one profession blinds us to research showing that each discipline attracts different kinds of people, performs research in widely differing ways, knows only certain fields and is quite ignorant about other areas, has different types of careers, and faces distinct problems of its own.

Not only does each profession have its own special knowledge, it also has its core work. While teaching takes most of a professor's time, it is published research which the profession rewards. In this way the academic professions differ from the service professions like law or dentistry; for the primary goal in academia is not the application of expert knowledge, but the creation of new knowledge. A study sponsored by the Carnegie Commission on Higher Education confirms what has been known for many decades: The professor who publishes in professional books or journals earns more, gets promoted faster, and works at a more "prestigious" institution. The true professionals, then, are those professors who do scholarship and publish, not those who primarily teach. If research activity is used as the measure of the professional, then two thirds of American faculty qualify. If publishing anything will do, then about half of American faculty are professionals. But if the professional is the person who steadily produces scholarly works, about 20 percent of the faculty belong to the academic professions. Thus, not only are there many distinct professions in higher education, but only a fraction of American faculty are true professionals—that is, research scholars who produce a substantial body of published work.

If scholarship is the core activity of the academic professions, teaching undergraduates is not. Despite all the arguments that scholarship gives teaching its lively edge and teaching puts narrow research into broad perspective, the two are in conflict for the professor's time and orientation. Research and graduate teaching are *professional* activities, while teaching undergraduates is an *institutional* activity. In nearly every poll of faculty, from state colleges to elite universities, professors are reported as wanting more time to do research or to teach graduate students in research, and less time for college teaching. Yet these faculty uniformly say they enjoy teaching. What is going on? Quite simply, the weight given to publications for salary increases and promotions, even at institutions where faculty publish little, is so great that professors feel compelled to take time from their teaching in order to advance themselves. They wish, however, that the quality of their teaching counted more toward advancement than it now does. At Stanford University, only 20 percent of the faculty believe that teaching greatly influences advancements, while 51 percent wish it did. At a nearby state university, 4 percent rated teaching as important for their career, but ten times that percentage wished it were. Here is a pathology of the American system —and not the American system alone—which tries to fuse brilliant, rare scholarship with universal, public education.

The injuries to students and faculty alike come from there being only one model of the successful professor. Our greatest need is to provide at least as many paths to distinction in academia as exist in the legal profession. There a person can aspire to be general counsel for IBM, a senior partner of a law firm, a professor of law, a distinguished judge, or a champion of citizens, like Ralph Nader. The legal profession honors all of these callings; each provides great rewards. For university faculty, the most obvious model besides the research scholar is the excellent teacher, but neither great nor less prominent institutions consistently reward this calling.

Alternate Models for Higher Education

Few realize that before this century began there were three models of the academic man and the institution in which he worked. All three shaped American higher education and are still important today for thinking about its purposes. First, the English or Oxford model of the eighteenth century emphasized mental discipline for a ruling elite. The implicit goal was to provide a common social, moral, and intellectual experience for sons of the elite. Here the professor served, above all, as a moral and intellectual teacher. Thus, a specific subject was not so important in itself as in the mental discipline it developed. Teaching provided an occasion for instilling moral and intellectual values. From the seventeenth through the nineteenth centuries, America's elite colleges and universities drew heavily on the Oxford model.

The second source of ideas about higher education came from Scotland, whose universities in the nineteenth century were public and open. Scotland already had an extraordinary literacy rate, higher than England's, and the Scottish approach to higher education fit nicely on the top of a broad base of public education. In contrast to the English at Oxford, the Scots emphasized practical subjects such as accounting and government. Consequently, they valued the professor for what he knew about a specific subject and the audiences he could draw. In a country like the United States, with its predominantly utilitarian view of public education, this concept of higher education and its faculty gained considerable influence. It signaled a curriculum and an organization entirely different from the Oxford model and best seen in the land-grant universities where practical subjects were offered to working adults all over the state by traveling teams of faculty. Nothing could differ more from the model of elite education.

The third ideal, of course, came from Germany. It emphasized scientific training—even in the nonsciences—and scientifically conducted research aimed at expanding knowledge. As an institution, the university served other functions, particularly to certify people in various pursuits so that they could enter respectable careers. But the heart of the university lay in scientific research. This model differed from the other two in its neglect of teaching, except for training future scientists. Unlike the other models, the chief activity was publishing research; thus it regarded the professor primarily as someone who discovered new frontiers of knowledge through research.

The German model transformed the faculty in the United States from a small group of men who shared the same education and intellectual heritage, regardless of which subject they taught, into a cluster of disciplinary professions, all eager to establish their own societies, journals, and distinctive identities. It altered the undergraduate curriculum. Charles Eliot "integrated" the old idea of undergraduate education with the new research thrust by allowing research faculty to offer any courses they wished and letting students choose among them. In reality, the elective system allowed faculty to teach their research specialties, leaving general education to chance.

Institutionally, this model usually mixed with one of the other two, creating research universities with elite, liberal arts colleges inside them or research universities with mass, utilitarian colleges and large extension efforts reaching out to farmers and businessmen. Although this "academic revolution" least affected private and denominational colleges, it nevertheless created an entirely new structure of prestige which slowly pushed most of the private and denominational colleges to the periphery. This one-dimensional status system also made institutions more competitive and thereby reduced diversity. The resulting stratification produced institutional mobility, as normal schools upgraded themselves to teachers' colleges, teachers' colleges to liberal arts colleges, the latter to regional universities, and these to national ones.

Problems Resulting from the Academic Professions

The demise of diversity has a specific character; it has resulted from the well-intentioned effort of institutions to acquire good reputations in a situation in which the academic professions have established only one standard of excellence. This homogenizing thrust behind institutional mobility also has something to do with the increased size of campuses and the general notion that bigger is better, more comprehensive. Bigness and prestige are related, because one must add on graduate programs to gain stature.

The price for these trends can be seen in Robert Pace's refreshing study *The Demise of Diversity?* It might also have been called *Celebration of the Liberal Arts College*. In measures of faculty and peer involvement, academic satisfaction, stimulating academic experiences, and meaningful campus life, the alumni and students of these colleges rate their experience one or two standard deviations above the alumni and students of comparable universities. These institutions do what educators dream a college should do. They make profound differences in the people who pass through them, not only in terms of the college experience but in terms of lasting breadth. On measures of broadened literary acquaintance, awareness of different philosophies and cultures, appreciation of art, music, and drama, friendships and social development, and the ability to write and speak effectively, the liberal arts colleges come out ahead. In particular, select colleges do noticeably better than select universities. Yet these institutions are now closing at a rapid rate.

The elective system, which treats each academic subject as equally worthy, was necessary; without it, the undergraduate curriculum could not have been reconciled with the full range of academic professions, each proud and devoted only to its fraction of knowledge. By the same token, subjects outside the disciplines do not exist academically and subjects between them create professional strains. This also explains the peculiar way in which universities respond to social problems. They do not fit neatly into one academic profession or another; often they do not lend themselves to journal articles. But one task of the academician, particularly someone building a career, is to *make* his or her work on a social problem count academically.

At the institutional rather than the individual level, this pattern has profoundly affected professional schools, which by definition are directly concerned with social problems. They, too, have been forced to play the only game in town—academic prestige—and this has meant that educators are trained by research scholars and lawyers by professors with equally little firsthand experience. Nathan Glazer has recently argued that the conflicts between practitioners and research faculty distinguish the schools of lesser professions like education, social work, the clergy, and city planning, from the schools of law and medicine. This assertion is simply inaccurate. The research-vs.-clinical debate has dominated law and medical schools in the past decade. The only way for the service professions to avoid the distortions of academic prestige is to hire the best practitioners to senior posts and give them control over much of professional training.

Policies for the Future

If the academic professions have generated not only some of education's greatest accomplishments, but also some of its major problems, is there a way to reduce the problems without diminishing the accomplishments as well? I think there is. Let us begin with an earlier observation— that only 20 percent of all faculty publish scholarship with any regularity. The other 80 percent have been studied and treated in the terms of this special minority, terms which simply do not fit. As a result, we know little about the careers, hopes, sources of satisfactions, and fears of these men and women. Instead we know that they do *not* publish, that they do *not* conduct sustained research, that they do *not* have light teaching loads, that they do *not* teach graduate students. We also know that, having no alternate model, they seek the professional ideals, a quest that can lead only to humiliation and a downgrading of their current, valuable work. . . .

Clearly what higher education needs in the years to come are alternate models of academic work. Given the complexity of this subject, let us take the simplest but most central model—the good, undergraduate teacher. Since teaching is basically an institutional and local enterprise, this model requires not $10,000 national awards for distinction, but careful assessments of teaching quality that affect promotions and salaries at each institution. Many people ask how the quality of teaching would be measured, but those who ask typically do not try to find out. Meanwhile, dozens of colleges and universities are evaluating their faculty as teachers in a serious way. The methods are flawed, though no more flawed than the methods for evaluating scholarly excellence, and they are improving with experience.

It is particularly important that such a reform become widespread in the next decade, because the tight job market will mean that graduate students trained to do research will filter down to colleges and universities that could not have attracted them before. They will carry with them the research model, and if left unchecked, will press these institutions to ape Harvard or Michigan. Given the limited pool of brilliance in any one generation, this will simply mean more second-rate scholarship and less devotion to teaching. Fortunately, pervading all faculty from great universities to lesser colleges is a demand that teaching count for more. This demand can reasonably be interpreted as widespread alienation; faculty at all levels do not like to spend large amounts of time doing something for which they are not rewarded. Either they want to do more of what counts, or they want what they do to count.

To make teaching an honored and influential calling in higher education, we must know much more about teaching faculty and their careers. One problem for both teaching and research faculty is that the career ladder ends when one becomes a professor at about age forty. There you are, Professor of Sociology, specializing in deviance and stratification, and you have twenty-five years to go. With each year it gets harder and more frightening to switch fields. Structurally this is a badly designed career, one encouraging defensive, stale people in the senior ranks.

This problem of career might well be linked to another, the professional obstacles to launching interdisciplinary programs. Such programs can stimulate faculty as well as students, and many reports on higher education have recommended them. If institutional funds are arranged in the right way, and if such ventures in education are rewarded locally, professors would have nothing to lose and everything to gain by entering a new venture. In short, if administrations put real clout behind excellent and imaginative teaching, and keep rewarding their faculty for doing so throughout their entire career, they will get what they bargain for. It is worth a try.

Anything grows from its beginnings, and the college professor begins as a graduate student. The shame of the graduate schools for years has been that they constrict the imagination and teach buoyant souls to plod. They also fail to train students in the work they will be doing most of their lives—teaching—at the same time that they train students in what only a few will do—research. Needless to say, there are great opportunities for growth in graduate schools, and with the job market so tight, perhaps they will do better. If one school made its graduates stand out from the rest by giving them excellent supervision in teaching, they would be given preference in the job market. Soon other graduate schools would follow suit.

In conclusion, major problems resulting from the structure of the academic professions can be overcome without injuring research. It must be recognized that 80 percent of all faculty do not contribute to scholarly excellence, while the other 20 percent devote considerable time to undergraduate instruction. Promising policies are those which realign rewards and programs to fit this reality and which create new models of excellence for what most faculty do already. In effect such policies would broaden the values of the academic professions and make their structure more flexible. Teaching has a local, client-centered quality which lends itself easily to a diversity of student needs and educational approaches that disciplines shaped by research alone cannot accommodate.

THE STRUGGLE OVER TENURE [3]

Academic tenure—the prevailing system of faculty job security—has been under fire for one reason or another ever since the concept was first formally introduced in 1915. The deteriorating economic situation now facing many American colleges has resulted in another and, in some ways, a more serious attack on the system. As long as the criticism of tenure focused primarily on the protection it afforded radicals or alleged subversives, or even incompetents, educators could defend the practice on the ground that its retention was essential for academic freedom. But in the last few years, as colleges and universities have been forced to economize and as many young Ph.D.s have been unable to find employment, it has been argued that academic freedom can be protected in ways other than the granting of a lifetime job.

The tenure question becomes increasingly bound up with faculty unionization, which has been described in *The Chronicle of Higher Education* ["Faculties at the Bargain-

[3] From "Academic Tenure," by Mary Costello, staff writer. *Editorial Research Reports.* v 1, no 9:163-9. Mr. 1, '74. Reprinted by permission.

ing Table," by P. W. Semas. p 9. N. 26, '73] as "on the threshold of becoming higher education's 'issue of the decade.' " Faculty unrest seems to be replacing the student unrest of a few years ago. And at no time of year is it more apparent than in the spring when teachers and administrators both must think about job needs and availability for next fall.

Noisy tenure battles already have erupted, among other places, at Southern Illinois University, Bloomfield (New Jersey) College, and the University of Wisconsin. Southern Illinois, beset by a 20 percent enrollment decline since 1970 and deep budget cuts, has ordered the dismissal by June 15 [1974] of 104 faculty and professional staff members, including 28 who hold tenure. Bloomfield, with a similar problem, has ordered tenure abolished and the faculty reduced from 72 to 52—an order that is being fought in court by the American Association of University Professors. In May 1973, the University of Wisconsin sent layoff notices to 88 tenured faculty members on nine of its campuses but later rescinded 19 of the notices.

Arguments against tenure focus on (1) its cost to the institution; and (2) its effects on the present and future job market in academia; and (3) on the quality of faculty performance. W. Todd Furniss of the American Council on Education calculated in 1973 that "a single grant of tenure represents a commitment by the institution of $1 million of its resources to the faculty member." If current tenure practices are continued and projections for declining college enrollment and fewer faculty openings are realized, it is argued, the cost might become intolerable for many financially hard-pressed schools.

Extent, Origins and Provisions of Tenure Status

Alan M. Carter, a senior fellow at the Carnegie Commission on Higher Education, has said that approximately 50 percent of the full-time faculty members in American colleges and universities have tenure. If the present pattern remains constant, he wrote, "we might expect as many as 72 percent of the faculty to hold tenure by 1990." This would mean "the virtual disappearance of the under-thirty-five group from the teaching profession." Another estimate is that the percentage of teachers with tenure could be as high as 90 percent by 1990.

Critics of tenure contend that many of the nation's most prestigious institutions are already becoming "tenured in," leaving little room for an infusion of new blood or flexible course planning. In 1972, 84 percent of the full-time faculty members at California Institute of Technology had tenure; 75 percent did at Stanford, while at Johns Hopkins and Northwestern the figure was 69 percent and at Yale 65 percent.

The Commission on Academic Tenure in Higher Education in March 1973 issued a report, *Faculty Tenure,* stating that "tenure plans are in effect in all public and private universities and public four-year colleges; in 94 percent of the private colleges; and in more than two thirds of the nation's two-year colleges, public and private. An estimated 94 percent of all faculty members in American universities and colleges are serving in institutions that confer tenure."

In 1940, the Association of American Colleges (AAC) and American Association of University Professors (AAUP) developed what has since become the standard tenure plan for institutions of higher learning. The 1940 Principles on Academic Freedom and Tenure and its subsequent interpretations and extensions had, by 1970, been endorsed by eighty-one organizations and adopted, officially or unofficially, by most American colleges.

Nevertheless, the commission found that there were "great variations in tenure policies and practices." These variations included "definition of tenure; its legal basis; criteria for appointment, reappointment and award of tenure; length of probationary period; categories of personnel eligible for tenure; relationship between tenure and rank; procedures for recommending appointment and awarding tenure; procedures for appeal from adverse decisions; procedures to be followed in dismissal cases; role of faculty, administration, students and governing board in personnel actions; methods of evaluating teachers, scholarship and public service; and retirement arrangements."

Fritz Machlup, in his presidential address at the 50th annual meeting of the AAUP in St. Louis on April 10, 1964, identified four types of tenure: (1) tenure by law, (2) by contract, (3) by moral commitment, and (4) by courtesy, kindness, timidity or inertia.

Tenure by law and tenure by contract can be enforced by the courts. Tenure by moral code can be enforced only by the pressure of moral forces, particularly by the threat of public condemnation ... Tenure without commitment ... may be only a tenuous tenure, but it is nevertheless real and practical: many members of the academic profession can expect to hold their positions indefinitely because administrative officers are nice, kind or lazy.

Candidates for law or contract tenure are judged, usually by college administrators after recommendations from colleagues and department chairmen, on what they accomplished during their probationary period, on how well they performed and on what they can be expected to do in the future. Studies indicate that in the past tenure has been awarded rather generously. A survey conducted for the Commission on Academic Tenure showed that over 80 percent of the candidates considered for tenure in 1971 were granted it. That year, 42 percent of the institutions awarded tenure to all candidates.

Academic Freedom as Basic Defense for Tenure

Once a teacher has been given tenure, it is extremely difficult for the college to get rid of him. The burden of proof for incompetence, unethical conduct or dire financial conditions is on the institution. The administration must present formal charges, usually before a group of the professor's colleagues, and generally allow the accused to have the benefit of counsel in all proceedings against him. If there is any doubt about the fairness of the dismissal, the teacher involved can appeal to the American Association of University Professors. If, after investigating, the AAUP finds that the college was unjust, it may be "censured"—association members are urged not to accept jobs at the college.

While several national commissions on college problems have criticized the tenure system as it now functions, they have recommended that it be reformed rather than abolished. In 1970, the President's Commission on Campus Unrest said:

Tenure has strong justification because of its role in protecting the academic freedom of senior faculty members. But it can also protect practices that detract from the institution's primary functions, that are unjust to students and that grant faculty members a freedom from accountability that would be unacceptable in any other profession.

Another 1970 report, this one by the Special Committee on Campus Tensions, said: "Tenure policies need to be appraised. . . . It sometimes has been a shield for indifference and neglect . . . of duties. . . ." Nevertheless, "Scholarly communities must be protected as effectively as tenure now protects individual professors." The most comprehensive of the studies, *Faculty Tenure* by the Commission on Academic Tenure, affirmed its belief in the concept of tenure but made forty-seven recommendations for improving present practices.

Those who wish to retain tenure or abolish it inevitably base their arguments on the relationship between academic freedom and tenure. Clark Byse and Louis Joughin, in their classic study *Tenure in American Higher Education* (1959), wrote: "The principal justification for academic tenure is that it enables a faculty member to teach, study and act free from a large number of restraints and pressures which otherwise would inhibit independent thought and action. . . ." The University of Utah Commission to Study

Tenure praised the system as a bastion of academic freedom in a report the commission issued in May 1971.

The Harvard University Committee on Governance has challenged the argument that abolition of tenure would improve teaching performance—at least at Harvard.

There is some reason to believe [the committee said] that the guarantee of tenure *at Harvard* has permitted the university to gather a quality faculty *on the cheap* and that it might cost Harvard *more*—simply in financial terms—were it forced to compete by way of annual short-term appointments with private industry....

Tenure may not guarantee an incompetent professor a permanent position, but it does make it difficult for a college to get rid of him. Dr. Thomas J. Truss, associate director of the AAUP, told *Editorial Research Reports* that dismissal for incompetence is very rare and that institutions generally negotiate an early retirement program for tenured professors who are physically or mentally unable to cope with their teaching assignments. Another method of disposing of tenure-holders is to eliminate the courses they teach. But neither early retirements nor the elimination of professional positions has elicited the controversy and notoriety that have greeted a handful of recent "dismissal with cause" cases.

Recent Cases Involving Job Rights

Probably the most publicized of these involved H. Bruce Franklin, a tenured associate professor of English at Stanford University. Franklin, a self-styled Maoist revolutionary, was charged by the university with inciting students to disrupt a scheduled speech, close down campus buildings, disobey police orders and engage in other disruptive conduct in violation of Stanford's 1967 Statement of Policy on Appointment and Tenure. The case was heard by an elected seven-member faculty tribunal beginning in late 1971. Early the next year, the members voted, 5 to 2, that Franklin be dismissed.

One of the strongest criticisms of the Franklin decision came from Alan M. Dershowitz of Harvard Law School. While saying that "Bruce Franklin's political views are despicable to me," Dershowitz wrote: "The dangerous precedent embodied in the Franklin decision will lie about like a loaded weapon ready to be picked up and used by any university administration, board of regents or state legislature wanting to rid itself of uncomfortable radicals. . . . His [Franklin's] right to advocate his program—even one that rests on violence—must be protected."

Dismissal with cause of tenured faculty members can be appealed and the institution is obliged to give the reasons for its decision and provide a hearing for the professor involved. There is generally far less legal protection for the nontenured teacher. According to the Commission on Academic Tenure, "when a probationary appointment is not renewed or when tenure is denied, nearly half (47 percent) of all institutions always provide written reasons for the action to the faculty member; 16 percent never give reasons. Procedures under which a faculty member may appeal a decision . . . are available in 87 percent of the institutions."

Controversy over the denial of tenure or renewal of contract to nontenured professors has centered on those refused appointment for what was deemed subversive or unconventional beliefs or behavior. In 1969, David E. Green, assistant professor of history at Ohio State University, was discharged from his post, despite a recommendation for leniency by the faculty committee, for burning his draft card and allegedly inciting students to violence. In 1970, the California Board of Regents refused to renew the contract of Angela Davis, the black militant and avowed Communist, as associate professor of philosophy. The same year, Jack H. Kurzweil, an assistant professor of electrical engineering at San Jose State College, was denied tenure because he was married to a Communist.

The Supreme Court in 1972 decided two cases involving

nontenured professors in public colleges who were contesting the nonrenewal of their contracts. The first concerned David F. Roth, a first-year assistant professor of political science at Wisconsin State University. Roth, who was given no reason for the decision not to rehire him and no opportunity to challenge it, claimed that the real reason for his dismissal was his criticism of university officials. The second case involved Robert P. Sindermann, a professor of government and social science at Odessa (Texas) Junior College, which has no formal tenure system. After publicly disagreeing with the institution's board of regents, he was denied a new contract for the 1969–70 school year. Sindermann, like Roth, was given no reason and no hearing.

In the *Roth* case, the Supreme Court ruled, 6 to 3, that teachers in state-run colleges who are employed on an annual contract do not have the right to a hearing when their contracts are not renewed unless they can show that they have a "property interest" in continued employment. In the *Sindermann* case, the Court held, again 6 to 3, that although a professor may not have formal tenure, he may have *de facto* tenure based on the policy at the particular institution. Sindermann's service at Odessa, the Court said, gave him the right to demonstrate his claim to continued employment at a hearing.

With regard to "property interests," the Court held in the *Roth* case that the Fourteenth Amendment's procedural protections cannot be invoked unless the facts show that the teacher already acquired interests in specific benefits. The *Sindermann* ruling added that the acquisition of interests subject to protection can be shown not only by formal rules or contracts but by agreements implied from words and conduct in light of the surrounding circumstances.

A PROGRAM FOR THE FUTURE [4]

The year 1932 was a troubled time for America. The country was shaken by a severe depression, unemployment was high, business was stagnant, and veterans of World War I, unable to find jobs, had encamped in Washington. The concept of a planned society in the USSR caused many Americans to question the free-enterprise system.

In February 1932 Professor George S. Counts startled the educational profession by his address to the annual convention of the Progressive Education Association (PEA), in which he asked, "Dare the schools build a new social order?" Counts left no doubt that he believed a new social order was necessary. He challenged the progressive schools because they were the most promising movement for change on the educational horizon. Counts contended that if schools were to build a new social order, they would have to drop their Deweyan child-centeredness, come to grips with planning an education for social change, cease to allow the individual child to do only what he wanted to do, and help young people to understand and cope with the problems of the times. In this way, schools would be building for a new social order.

The boldness of Counts's address startled the conference and stirred delegates deeply. The dinner meeting ended with groups forming and talking—some of them discussing Counts's challenge into the wee hours of the morning. In the history of education no other speech has had such an impact on the educational profession.

But how do schools go about building a new social order? Counts was not specific as to how it should be done or what the curriculum should be. He was even less specific about the new social order, except that privilege was to be stripped from the few and that democratic planning would create a

⁴ From "A Call to the Educators of America," by Frederick L. Redefer, professor emeritus, higher education, New York University Saturday/Review World. 1:49-50. Jl. 27, '74. Reprinted by permission.

society with low unemployment, better housing, and better health.

The PEA had no ready answers to the questions Counts raised, and the debate that ensued divided the movement as to whether a new social order could be achieved through education without indoctrination, or whether, if teachers resorted to indoctrination, they would cease to be educators.

A committee issued "A Call to the Teachers of America," written largely by Counts; but by 1936, when this report was submitted to the members for study, the New Deal, under Roosevelt's leadership, was tackling more vigorously the problems of unemployment, housing, and the welfare of the people. As a result, it became clear that the schools would not attempt to build a new social order.

The educational situation today is not too different from that of 1932, although our problems are not solely economic. They still include not only housing and health but also overpopulation; pollution of air, sea, and land; the wanton destruction of the earth's resources; war; and/or atomic annihilation. What is new about today's critical problems is that none of them can be solved on a national basis. Our international organizations are not equipped to tackle them when the minds of statesmen and citizens are still nationally provincial.

Higher education has not educated youth for this new world. A few professors in individual courses facing the present and future have reached a small percentage of the total student body. These scattered courses do not add up to much, and colleges, whose major concern is the professional preparation of students, have expressed little interest in the crisis mankind faces. Without the challenge of what a new world could be like, students become socially apathetic.

The challenge to higher education presented by Ivan Illich's *Deschooling Society*, in which he proposed that all schools and colleges be closed, has not been taken seriously. The revolt of college students of the fifties and sixties produced little fundamental change. Pass/fail grades in place of the old marking system have not brought change in the curriculum. Student-organized courses, enjoying a brief flurry of interest, have been submerged by faculty power. "Universities without walls" show little concern with the problems of mankind. The voluminous study of higher education conducted by the Carnegie Foundation inspired no purpose for higher education other than supporting the status quo, while the grants of the Ford Foundation have sidestepped any fundamental change. American education faces a world situation that it seems unwilling to look at, and today it is higher education, rather than childhood education, that needs to be challenged to build a new world order.

"A State of Educational Chaos"

Higher education is in a crisis far more complex than mere lack of funds. The loss of faith in our colleges and universities as agencies for social improvement is clearly evident in the apathy of students, and a "withdrawal" is spreading in an expressed cynicism among graduate students. Robert Maynard Hutchins has given up reforming higher education and calls for reforming society first. But does this not require a better-educated citizenry and a different education *among the faculty itself?* Colleges no longer express an educational effort to achieve definite purposes.

In the past two decades the traditional program of liberal arts in undergraduate education has crumbled—a victim of graduate school specialization, of emphasis on excessive vocationalism, and of the revolt of youth against any restrictive requirements. A state of educational chaos has resulted. This is particularly true for the first two years of the traditional four-year college. These years no longer have meaning for students. Advanced standing and early admission of students indicate that these years are no longer considered essential for education, even by the faculty. In most colleges these are the years to be avoided for teaching assignments by the more experienced professors. More and more colleges have become a "holding operation," and they do little for young people and contribute less to society as a whole.

Are colleges and faculties ready for change? The answer is no, because faculties are participants in a built-in system protecting the time-encrusted administrative arrangements and practices of higher education that inhibit change.

There are, however, pockets of younger and older teachers who realize that change is necessary. The world confrontation, the shock of Watergate, the lack of ethics in high places, and the commercialization of American culture have convinced some that a new education is necessary if we are to educate a younger generation that is concerned, committed, and prepared to create a better society. These pockets of educational leadership need to be discovered, encouraged, and supported. If given encouragement, they could create a purpose for higher education.

A new purpose for higher education must be directed toward the future, making students aware of the dangers of the present drift; the crucial shortages the world will face in energy, resources, foods; the effects of overpopulation; pollution of water and land as projected in the recent report by the Club of Rome. Higher education must prepare students for a life far simpler than they now live, for satisfactions less dependent on technological machines.

Such a purpose requires design and experimentation to create the kind of man needed by the world into which we are moving so rapidly. The traditional liberal arts are no longer relevant to this end. Rational thought needs to be applied to daily living, and a knowledge of the past must be applied to contemporary problems. An education limited to the study of the Western world is an anachronism. The traditional courses of the history of Western civilization, the appreciation of Western art, Western music, and Western literature omit more than half of the world of man. It is such courses, repeating what is sketched in secondary schools, that have helped to turn students off, causing them to drop out in order to discover who they are. The new approaches in anthropology, economics, geology, and international relations need to be brought together in new patterns. The East and West need not be separated in courses or departments. Interdisciplinary designs are necessary if students are to receive the background essential for informed citizens of the world. Before one becomes a lawyer, a doctor, a business executive, or a teacher, one needs to be a *man*—who knows himself and others, who thinks of himself as a man before he thinks of himself as a citizen of any particular country, or an example of any racial strain, or as a member of any religious or nonreligious group. He needs to be a man prepared to live and share with others the planet earth and to be vitally concerned about the destruction of any man or any part of that earth. It is clearly evident that such men are not plentiful today and even more evident that educators do not do what they could to develop such men.

A Lesson from the Depression

Educators would do well to reexamine the successful project sponsored by the Progressive Education Association in the depression years (1932–41) known as The Eight-Year Study.

This study approached the problem of college admission with a view to freeing secondary schools to plan a better educational program and, at the same time, to prepare students for college. It aimed at breaking up the rigid plan for college admission based on grades received and examinations passed in required subjects. For eight years practically all colleges in the United States allowed thirty secondary schools freedom from specific college-admission requirements. They were free to plan a new education for youth.

The Eight-Year Study was one of the few successful experiments in American education, and it demonstrated there is no *one* way of preparing for college. It proved that a variety of patterns could be followed and that graduates of the participating schools achieved as high a level of success in college as did matched students from schools following traditional courses. Unfortunately, World War II, the flood of GIs into our colleges in the postwar years, the tremendous expansion of higher education, the fears of communism of the McCarthy era—all contributed to lessening the benefits that should have been derived from this study. Most unfortunately, the colleges of the thirties concluded—from the examples of these young people who had been educated differently—that there was little need for change.

America is now questioning its values and is more aware than ever before that changes must come. Is this not the time to develop purposes for education and to create a new education for some students in some schools and colleges by some of the faculty? Is it not a time when a social purpose for education can be found and a commitment to an improved world accepted? Must we wait for society to change before colleges do?

A new eight-year study involving *secondary schools and colleges* is needed. It should focus on the first two years of college, before specialization sets in, and on the last two years of the secondary school—periods that are now floundering. Faculties of colleges and secondary schools should plan together for four years of education with an arrangement for admission to college similar to that which existed in the original Eight-Year Study. Such a proposal of a "new" four-year unit has been made before and has a sound psychological basis in the stage of development of young people.

A national committee could explore such a proposal with the college and secondary-school associations that now exist in the eight geographical regions of the United States to discover their interest in establishing an eight-year study in their respective areas. Wherever there is an interest, a committee could be established in each region to contact the faculties of colleges and secondary schools and to select those that are prepared to participate. What one region designs for such an education need not be identical with what another region plans, nor does it follow that what a college does in its first two years or what a secondary school does in its last two years would be similar to what all other schools and colleges in that region are doing. Designs for the education of man living on the planet earth ought to produce diversity, for there must be many paths to this goal. Regional committees could select the most promising college and secondary-school plans and be responsible for communication among the participating institutions to improve, evaluate, and advance plans in the course of eight years.

A single foundation need not support this proposal, but many of them cooperatively could make such a project possible. The original Eight-Year Study, involving thirty schools, required a grant of less than $2 million over eight years. This proposal might call for $20 million over an eight-year span, and this is a small amount to devote to meet the needs of American education.

The creativeness of educators can meet the challenge if innovative colleges and imaginative teachers are sought out—rather than those merely with reputations and status. In this spirit, the educators of America are summoned to answer the challenge of this age and to create an education for the man who must build a new world order.

BIBLIOGRAPHY

An asterisk (*) preceding a reference indicates that the article or a part of it has been reprinted in this book.

Books, Pamphlets, and Documents

Aptheker, Bettina. The academic rebellion in the United States. Citadel Press. '72.

Astin, A. W. The college environment. American Council on Education. 1785 Massachusetts Ave. N.W. Washington, D.C. 20036. '68.

Astin, A. W. Predicting academic performance in college: selectivity data for 2300 American colleges. Free Press. '71.

Astin, A. W. and Panos, R. J. The educational and vocational development of college students. American Council on Education. 1785 Massachusetts Ave. N.W. Washington, D.C. 20036. '69.

Astin, H. S. and others. Higher education and the disadvantaged student. Human Service Press. 4301 Connecticut Ave. N.W. Washington, D.C. 20008. '72.

Baldridge, J. V. Power and conflict in the university. Wiley. '71.

Ben-David, Joseph. American higher education: directions old and new. McGraw-Hill. '71.

Bereday, G. Z. F. Towards the university for the masses: North America, USSR, Japan, Europe. Jossey-Bass. '73.

Berg, Ivar. Education and jobs: the great training robbery. Beacon Press. '71.

Bernard, Jessie. Academic women. Meridian. '74.

Bird, Caroline. The case against college; ed. by Helene Mandelbaum. McKay. '75.

Byse, Clark and Joughin, Louis. Tenure in American higher education; plans, practices, and the law. Cornell University Press. '59.

Cahn, S. M. The eclipse of excellence; a critique of American education. Public Affairs Press. '73.

Carnegie Commission on Higher Education. Governance of higher education; 6 priority problems: a report and recommendations. McGraw-Hill. '73.

Carnegie Commission on Higher Education. The more effective use of resources. McGraw-Hill. '72.

Carnegie Commission on Higher Education. Priorities for action. McGraw-Hill. '73.

207

Carnegie Commission on Higher Education. Reform on campus: changing students, changing academic programs. McGraw-Hill. '72.

Caws, Peter and Ripley, S. D. The bankruptcy of academic policy; ed. by P. C. Ritterbush. Acropolis Books. '72.

*Committee for Economic Development. The management and financing of colleges; a statement by the Research and Policy Committee, October 1973. The Committee. 477 Madison Ave. New York 10022. '73.

Dugger, Ronnie. The invaded universities: form, reform and new starts; a nonfiction play for 5 stages. Norton. '74.
  Excerpt. Harper's Magazine. 248:70-4+. Mr. '74. Counting house of academe.

Dykes, A. R. Faculty participation in academic decision making; report of a study. American Council on Education. 1785 Massachusetts Ave. N.W. Washington, D.C. 20036. '68.

Eurich, A. C. ed. Campus 1980: the shape of the future in American higher education. Dial Press. '68.

Eurich, Nell and Schwenkmeyer, Barry. Great Britain's open university: first chance, second chance, or last chance. Academy for Educational Development, Inc. 680 Fifth Ave. New York 10019. '71.

Feldman, S. D. Escape from the doll's house: women in graduate and professional school education; a report prepared for the Carnegie Commission on Higher Education. McGraw-Hill. '74.

Foster, Julian and Long, Durward, eds. Protest! student activism in America. Morrow. '69.

Gallagher, B. G. Campus in crisis. Harper. '74.

Gordon, M. S. ed. Higher education and the labor market. McGraw-Hill. '74.

Graubard, S. R. and Balotti, G. A. eds. The embattled university. Braziller. '70.

Greer, Colin. The Great School legend: a revisionist interpretation of American public education. Basic Books. '72.

Handlin, Oscar and Handlin, M. F. The American college and the American culture; socialization as a function of higher education. McGraw-Hill. '70.

Hansen, W. L. and Weisbrod, B. A. Benefits, costs and finance of public higher education. Markham. '69.

Harnett, R. T. College and university trustees: their backgrounds, roles and educational attitudes. Educational Testing Service. 20 Nassau St. Princeton, N.J. 08540. '69.

Hartman, R. W. Credit for college; public policy for student loans: a report for the Carnegie Commission on Higher Education. McGraw-Hill. '71.

Hodgkinson, H. L. and Meeth, L. R. eds. Power and authority [transformation of campus governance]. Jossey-Bass. '71.

Hoffman, Abbie. Revolution for the hell of it. Dial Press. '68.

Hofstadter, Richard and Hardy, C. D. The development and scope of higher education in the United States. Columbia University Press (for the Commission on Financing Higher Education). '52.

Hook, Sidney. Academic freedom and academic anarchy. Cowles. '70.

Illich, Ivan. Deschooling society. Harper. '71.

Jencks, Christopher and Riesman, David. The academic revolution. Doubleday. '68.

Jerome, Judson. Culture out of anarchy; the reconstruction of American higher learning. Herder & Herder. '70.

Kavanaugh, R. E. The grim generation. Pocket Books. '71.

Ladd, D. R. Change in educational policy. McGraw-Hill. '70.

Light, D. W. Jr. and others. The impact of the "academic revolution" on faculty careers. American Association for Higher Education. 1 Dupont Circle N.W. Washington, D.C. 20036. '72.

Lipset, S. M. Rebellion in the university. Little. '72.

Lipset, S. M. ed. Student politics. Basic Books. '67.

Livesey, Herbert. The professors. Charterhouse. '75.

Medsker, L. L. and Tillery, Dale. Breaking the access barriers; a profile of two-year colleges. McGraw-Hill. '71.

Michener, J. A. Kent State: what happened and why. Random House. '71.

Miller, S. M. and Roby, P. P. The future of inequality. Basic Books. '70.

Mosteller, Frederick and Moynihan, D. P. eds. On equality of educational opportunity; papers deriving from the Harvard University faculty seminar on the Coleman report. Vintage. '72.

Newcomer, Mabel. A century of higher education for American women. Harper. '59.

Newman, Frank and others. Report on higher education. U.S. Department of Health, Education, and Welfare. Washington, D.C. 20201. '71.

Nichols, D. C. and Mills, Olive, eds. The campus and the racial crisis. American Council on Education. 1785 Massachusetts Ave. N.W. Washington, D.C. 20036. '70.

Novak, Michael. The rise of the unmeltable ethnics; politics and culture in the seventies. Macmillan. '72.

Pace, C. R. The demise of diversity? a comparative profile of eight institutions. Carnegie Commission on Higher Education. 2150 Shattuck Ave., Berkeley, Calif. 94704. '74.

Parsons, Talcott and others. The American university. Harvard University Press. '73.

Regents Advisory Council for New York City. A regional plan for higher education: a report from New York City. New York State Education Department. Washington Ave. Albany, N.Y. 12224. '72.

Riesman, David and Stadtman, V. A. eds. Academic transformation; 17 institutions under pressure. McGraw-Hill (for the Carnegie Commission on Higher Education). '73.

Rogers, C. R. Freedom to learn; a view of what education might become. Merrill. '69.

Rolling Stone, Editors of. The age of paranoia. Pocket Books. '72.

Rossi, A. S. and Calderwood, Ann, eds. Academic women on the move. Russell Sage. '73.

Roszak, Theodore, ed. The dissenting academy. Random House. '68.

Rudolph, Frederick. The American college and university. Knopf. '62.

Salk, J. E. The survival of the wisest. Harper. '73.

Sanford, Nevitt, ed. The American college; a psychological and social interpretation of higher learning. Wiley. '62.

Sarason, S. B. The culture of the school and the problem of change. Allyn. '71.

Schein, Edgar. Professional education: some new directions. McGraw-Hill. '72.

Schultz, T. W. The economic value of education. Columbia University Press. '63.

Searle, J. R. The campus war; a sympathetic look at the university in agony. World. '71.

Sizer, T. R. Places for learning, places for joy: speculations on American school reform. Harvard University Press. '73.

Smelser, N. J. and Almond, G. A. eds. Public higher education in California. University of California Press. '74.

Taubman, Paul and Wales, Terence. Mental ability and higher educational attainment in the 20th century. National Bureau of Economic Research, Inc. 261 Madison Ave. New York 10016. '72.

Touraine, Alain. The academic system in American society. McGraw-Hill. '74.

Trent, J. W., and Medsker, L. L. Beyond high school: a psycho-sociological study of 10,000 high school graduates. Jossey-Bass. '68.

United States. President's Science Advisory Committee. Panel on Youth. Youth: transition to adulthood; report: James S. Coleman [and others]. Univ. of Chicago Press. '74.

Wallerstein, I. M. University in turmoil; the politics of change. Atheneum. '69.

Wallerstein, I. M. and Starr, Paul, eds. The university crisis reader. Random House. '71. 2v.

Wilson, Logan. Shaping American higher education. American Council on Education. 1785 Massachusetts Ave. N.W. Washington, D.C. 20036. '71.

Wolff, R. P. The ideal of the university. Beacon Press. '69.

PERIODICALS

AAUP Bulletin. 59:286-323. S. '73. The politics of public higher education; Illinois, by S. K. Gove and C. E. Floyd; Nebraska, by C. R. McKibbin; Wisconsin, by Allan Rosenbaum; Ohio, by J. B. Tucker.

AAUP Bulletin. 59:339-45. S. '73. Reviewing tenure. W. J. Kilgore.

AAUP Journal. 67:1-26. N. '73. Higher education—a quiet revolution for the 70s.

AAUP Journal. 67:17-20. N. '73. Women in higher education; a progress report. Bernice Sandler.

America. 131:75. Ag. 24, '74. Small revolt in the land of tenure. J. W. Donohue.

American Education. 9:28. Je. '73. Women's studies course: a personal experience. James Sheehy.

American Education. 10:31-4. Je. '74. Sampling college; project at Bay de Noc community college, Escanaba, Mich. E. E. Wuehle.

American Scholar. 42:569-92. Autumn '73. One's own primer of academic politics. Pandarus (pseudonym).

American West. 11:10-17+. Ja. '74. Confrontation and innovation on the campus. R. G. Lillard.

*Annals of the American Academy of Political and Social Science. 404:1-245. N. '72. American higher education: prospects and choices. R. D. Lambert, ed.
   Reprinted in this volume: American higher education in historical perspective. W. W. Brickman. p 31-44.

Annals of the American Academy of Political and Social Science. 409:125-34. S. '73. Education and equality. R. J. Staaf and Gordon Tullock.

*Better Homes and Gardens. 51:144+. My. '73. Ten common myths about college.

Better Homes and Gardens. 51:12+. N. '73. Home study: how it can pay off in college credits. G. M. Knox.

Business Week. p 122+. D. 8, '73. Columbia joins the "ivy college" turnaround; balancing the budget.

Business Week. p 143. Mr. 9, '74. Not many jobs for well-rounded
    college grads.
Changing Times. 27:4. Jl. '73. Job outlook for college grads: now
    to 1980.
Changing Times. 28:4. Jl. '74. College bills to pay? Brace yourself.
Christian Century. 91:491-2. My. 8, '74. Affirmative action and the
    Defunis case.
Christianity Today. 18:16-18. My. 24, '74. Should you go to college?
    Elisabeth Elliot.
Clearing House. 48:277. Ja. '74. Professing professors; professors of
    education. D. R. Macbeth.
*Commentary. 55:37-47. F. '73. Higher education for all? the case
    of open admissions. Martin Mayer.
Commonweal. 98:26. Mr. 16, '73. Balancing enrollments; plight
    of the private college and university.
Commonweal. 100:102+. Ap. 5, '74. Against affirmative action.
    Michael Novak.
*Daedalus. 103:25-32. Fall '74. Reflections on a worn-out model.
    Charles Frankel.
*Daedalus. 103:258-63. Fall '74. Thinking about faculty. Donald
    Light, Jr.
*Editorial Research Reports. v 1, no 9:163-80. Mr. 1, '74. Aca-
    demic tenure. Mary Costello.
Editorial Research Reports. v 2, no 9:663-80. College recruiting.
    Sandra Stencel.
*Education Digest. 38:12-15. Mr. '73. Who should go to college?
    Paul Woodring.
        Condensed from: Who Should Go to College. Phi Delta Kappa Educational
        Foundation. P.O. Box 789. Bloomington, Ind. 47401. '72. p 7-11, 35-8.
Education Digest. 38:26-9. Ap. '73. Open door versus the revolving
    door. T. M. Miller.
Education Digest. 39:67. N. '73. Higher tuition charges?
Education Digest. 39:50-2. D. 73. Standards, of course. M. S.
    Marshall.
*Education Digest. 39:57-9. My. '74. College student cohabitation.
    J. L. Morrison and Scott Anderson.
        Condensed from: College Student Journal. 7:14-19. N.-D. '73.
Education Digest. 40:17-20. S. '74. Future course of higher educa-
    tion. Clark Kerr.
Education Digest. 40:44-6. S. '74. Financing private colleges. Albert
    Berney.
Esquire. 82:93-4+. S. '74. New myth on campus. Roger Rapoport.
*Esquire. 82:102+. S. '74. College: dumbest investment of all.
    Caroline Bird and S. G. Necel.
Forbes. 114:37-8+. S. 15, '74. Coming shakeout in higher educa-
    tion: shortage of students.

*Fortune. 90:122-5+. S. '74. Everything is shrinking in higher education. Martin Mayer.

Good Housekeeping. 179:164. Ag. '74. Different ways to meet the high cost of college.

Harper's Magazine. 249:8-9. S. '74. Compulsory change; the Hastings College of Law policy of hiring retired professors. Dorothy Winter.

Intellect. 101:294-6. F. '73. Academic standards: pro and con. C. H. Moore.

Intellect. 101:371-3+. Mr. '73. Our newly developing wastelands: the American colleges. L .J. Lefkowitz.

Intellect. 102:9. O. '73. Coeducation and women's colleges.

Intellect. 102:96-7. N. '73. To evaluate a dean. J. R. Hoyle.

Intellect. 102:278-9. F. '74. Problems of private universities.

Intellect. 102:315-17. F. '74. Performance of college presidents. D. H. Bergquist.

Intellect. 102:344-5. Mr. '74. Case for women's colleges.

Intellect. 102:424-5. Ap. '74. Myth of change in higher education. C. W. Burnett.

Intellect. 102:426-7. Ap. '74. Three-year degree: what will it cost? C. N. Walker.

Journal of Higher Education. 45:285-95. Ap. '74. Moral man and immoral academy? leaves from the notebook of a tamed cynic. R. W. Friedrichs.

McCall's. 100:65. F. '73. Is the SAT failing?

McCall's. 100:38. Je. '73. Instant college credits for your life experience. Anne Staffin.

McCall's. 101:83+. Ap. '74. Why young people are turning away from casual sex. Kenneth Woodward and Betty Woodward.

Mademoiselle. 76:116-17+. Ja. '73. Does your college owe you a job? N. A. Comer.

Mademoiselle. 78:122-3+. F. '74. Do women's colleges need men? A. M. Cunningham.

Mademoiselle. 79:212-14+. Ag. '74. Five college cooperation: Amherst, Hampshire, U. of Massachusetts, Smith, Mount Holyoke. N. A. Comer

Mademoiselle. 79:297. Ag. '74. Unrevolution on the American campus. J. S. Faier.

Monthly Labor Review. 96:41-50. F. '73. Employment of recent college graduates. V. C. Perrella.

Ms. 2:101-2. Je. '74. Grading the college of your choice. M. C. Dunkle.

Ms. 2:102. Je. '74. Women's studies: looking for a degree?

Ms. 3:45-7. S. '74. Making of a Vassar man. Michael Wolff.

Nation. 216:206-10. F. 12, '73. Open admissions: a pilgrim's progress. Peter Sourian.

*Nation. 216:781-5. Je. 18, '73. No retreat from commitment. S. R. Weissman.

National Review. 26:470-1. Ap. 26, '74. College financial crisis.

National Review. 26:1166. O. 11, '74. Does student power corrupt? Edward Le Comte.

New Leader. 56:10-12. O. 29, '73. The inequities of academic tenure. D. M. Oshinsky.

New Republic. 169:19-21. O. 27, '73. Money on campus; the latest student unrest. Eliot Marshall.

*New Republic. 169:11-13. D. 29, '73. College cost squeeze: tuition controversy. Larry Van Dyne.

New Republic. 171:18-19. Jl. 27, '74. Confessions of an academic administrator.

*New York Times. p 19. D. 25, '73. "New vocationalism" now campus vogue. Iver Peterson.

New York Times. p 40. Ja. 20, '74. Antioch, a symbol of quality, struggling to survive. Evan Jenkins.

New York Times. p 43. F. 3, '74. Minorities drop in U.S. colleges. G. I. Maeroff.

New York Times. p 37. F. 5, '74. Class war over tuition. F. M. Hechinger.

New York Times. p 1+. F. 24, '74. At Brown, trend is back to grades and tradition. Robert Reinhold.

New York Times. p E 5. Mr. 3, '74. The legality of racial quotas. Anthony Lewis.

New York Times. p 21. Mr. 6, '74. Colleges urged to curb tenure to avoid inflexibility in staffs. G. I. Maeroff.

New York Times. p 1+. Mr. 31, '74. Colleges shift to hard sell in recruiting of students. Evan Jenkins.

New York Times. p 1+. Ap. 8, '74. Basis for college student aid is periled. G. I. Maeroff.

New York Times. p 21. Ap. 30, '74. Harvard study finds some benefits in temporarily dropping out of college. G. I. Maeroff.

New York Times. p 1+. My. 5, '74. The next freshman class: shifting pattern. Iver Peterson.

New York Times. p 1+. Je. 28, '74. Minority hiring said to hurt colleges. G. I. Maeroff.

New York Times. p 1+. S. 7, '74. Colleges face year of economic worry. G. I. Maeroff.

New York Times. p. 47. N. 7, '74. College textbooks being simplified to meet the needs of the poor reader. Iver Peterson.

New York Times. p. 47. N. 7, '74. Forecast of 23% drop in college rolls in state by 1990 stirs a controversy. E. B. Fiske.

New York Times. p 39. N. 20, '74. Facing facts in Ph.D. programs. G. I. Maeroff.

*New York Times p 1+. D. 1, '74. Fraternities reviving on a serious note. E. B. Fiske.

New York Times. p 37. Ap. 16, '75. Panel says 1 in 10 campuses will merge or shut in 5 years. Robert Reinhold.

New York Times. Sec 13. My. 4, '75. Spring survey of education.

*New York Times Magazine. p 14-15+. F. 10, '74. Unquiet quiet on campus. Ronald Berman.

New Yorker. 50:27. Ap. 1, '74. Notes and comment; Heliotrope, the open university of San Francisco.

Newsweek. 82:109-10. N. 12, '73. Frat is back.

Newsweek. 82:75. N. 26, '73. Pruning the perennials.

Newsweek. 83:32. Mr. 11, '74. Campus snapshot. K. I. Lansner.

Newsweek. 83:15. Je 3, '74. Intellectual taxicab company. Peter Carlson.

Newsweek. 83:59. Je. 17, '74. Pipers of Hamline; Hamline university's novel fund raising idea.

PTA Magazine. 67:18-19. bibliog (p 39) Ja. '73. Is the small college right for your child? H. M. Grutzmacher, Jr.

PTA Magazine. 67:30-3. bibliog (p 36) My. '73. Case against college; debunking a myth [with study-discussion program, by E. B. De Franco]. Rebecca Larsen.

PTA Magazine. 68:2. My. '74. Happenings in education: in what ways did the freshman of '73 differ from freshmen of past years? R. M. Levey.

Parents Magazine. 49:60-2+. F. '74. Plan-ahead program for college-bound youngsters. C. R. Clucas.

Progressive. 38:40-1. My. '74. Case of thoughtcrime: dismissal of G. Cooper from the University of Arkansas at Little Rock. Gene Lyons.

Progressive. 38:36. S. '74. Justice delayed; acquittal of Robert Brown in Vietnam protest case at California State College, Sonoma. Paul Berger.

Psychology Today. 8:22+. Jl. '74. The learning center—where the student is king; American university. Jack Horn.

Psychology Today. 8:72-6+. S. '74. What does college do for a person? frankly very little [interview, ed. by C. Tavris]. T. M. Newcomb.

Ramparts. 12:27-30+. Ap. '74. Could Karl Marx teach economics in America? L. S. Lifshultz.

*Reader's Digest. 105:107-12. Jl. '74. Sports recruiting: a college crisis.
  Condensed from New York Times. Mr. 10-15, '74. [series of stories by staff writers]

Reader's Digest. 105:123-5. S. '74. Reducing college costs. B. R. Anderson.

Saturday Review of Education. 1:54-5. F. '73. Out-of-staters: the tuition issue. John Mathews.

Saturday Review of Education. 1:25-7. Mr. '73. Can you make it into college in 1973? Test yourself on the college boards.

Saturday Review/World. 1:48-9. Mr. 9, '74. Are college trustees obsolete? J. F. Budd, Jr.

Saturday Review/World. 1:55-6. Ap. 6, '74. Colleges in search of freshmen. F. M. Hechinger.

Saturday Review/World. 1:68-70. My. 4, '74. Beyond the SATs: a whole-person catalog that works? Benjamin DeMott.

*Saturday Review/World. 1:49. Je. 1, '74. Experiment with radical reform [new curriculum at Brown University]. James Cass.

*Saturday Review/World. 1:49-50. Jl. 27, '74. Call to the educators of America. F. L. Redefer.

Science. 179:1081. Mr. 16, '73. Enclaves of pluralism: the private universities. Norman Hackerman.

Science. 181:897. S. 7, '73. University or knowledge factory. H. L. Enarson.
    Adapted from commencement address, University of New Mexico, May 1973.

Science. 182:697-8. N. 16, '73. Higher education: study urges altered thrust in federal support. Constance Holden.

Science. 184:537-42. My. 3, '74. Educational challenges for the university. Frederick Reif.

Science Digest. 76:72-6. Jl. '74. Silly season at M.I.T. Gurney Williams, 3d.

Senior Scholastic. 102:6-8. Ap. 2, '73. What? More school? Why not?

Seventeen. 32:46. D. '73. Maybe you shouldn't go away to college. Jack Cohen.

Social Science. 49:33-8. Winter '74. College youth and politics: the move from political to personal concerns. D. B. German.

Society. 11:89-91. Mr. '74. Constraint and variety of American education. P. G. Altbach.

Sports Illustrated. 40:86-90+. Je. 10; 24-8+. Je. 17. '74. 427: a case in point. Ray Kennedy.

Time. 103:72. My. 6, '74. Return of the campus recruiter.

Time. 103:117. My. 13, '74. Shopping for college; college fairs.

Time. 103:80. My. 27, '74. Alums are restless.

Today's Health. 50:68-9. O. '72. Let's make civility and discipline required courses of action at the nation's colleges. W. V. Shannon.

U.S. News & World Report. 73:43-4+. My. 21, '73. Latest plan to save colleges; pool books, labs, computers.

U.S. News & World Report. 74:43-6. Ap. 23, '73. Empty seats in colleges, end of a 20-year boom.

U.S. News & World Report. 76:68. F. 4, '74. Switch for student activists, working inside the system; public-interest research groups.

U.S. News & World Report. 76:53-4. Ap. 15, '74. Campus scene: now, it's buyer's choice.

*U.S. News & World Report. 76:39-40. My. 6, '74. Report card on all those campus reforms of the '60s.

U.S. News & World Report. 76:60. My. 6, '74. Bias against whites, effect of Court action.

*U.S. News & World Report. 77:42. Jl. 22, '74. College grads vs. others: earnings more than double.

U.S. News & World Report. 77:53-4. Jl. 22, '74. Minority hiring again a big issue for colleges.

U.S. News & World Report. 77:41-2. S. 23, '74. Good news for students, parents.

U.S. News & World Report. 77:56+. O. 14, '74. Struggle to pay for college—how four families manage it.

UNESCO Courier. 27:31-3+. F. '74. What's up in higher education? V. G. Onushkin and Antony Brock.

Vital Speeches of the Day. 39:727-32. S. 15, '73. Evaluating institutional performance; address. J. M. Bevan.

Vital Speeches of the Day. 40:154-9. D. 15, '73. Non-traditional studies; address, October 31, 1973. E. B. Nyquist.

*Vital Speeches of the Day. 40:396-8. Ap. 15, '74. What's left on campus to govern? address delivered before the American Association for Higher Education, Chicago, March 11, 1974. H. L. Enarson.

Vital Speeches of the Day. 40:493-7. Je. 1, '74. Deterioration of a college degree; address delivered at the Mexican Institute of Culture, Mexico City. April 29, 1974. W. J. McGill.

Vital Speeches of the Day. 40:588-91. Jl. 15. '74. Hazards of equality; commencement address, Hartford (Connecticut) College for Women, June 1, 1974. M. L. Thibeault.

Vital Speeches of the Day. 40:729-31. S. 15, '74. In pursuit of purpose; goals for American colleges; commencement address, Columbia (South Carolina) College, August 16, 1974. H. H. Parker.

Wall Street Journal. p 16. Ap. 25, '74. Over-educated. A. L. Otten.

Wall Street Journal. p 1+. My. 28, '74. The cost of living: family
    with $22,000 a year is squeezed by college expenses. T. P.
    Brown.
Washington Monthly. 6:30-9. Ap. '74. New hope for parents—a
    way to beat the costs of college. Walter Shapiro.